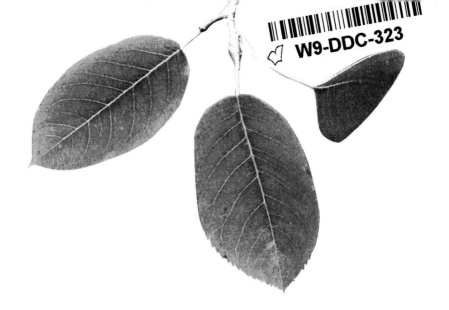

I am Keats as you are

poetry and writings

Glenn Peirson

Edited by: Mary Peirson and Ellyn Peirson

Printed in Canada

ISBN 9780986741104

FIN 16 11 10

2003

This book is dedicated to
Theodora Frances and Henry Oswald Peirson
for their future understanding of their father,
for a personal insight into his mind when they are adults,
and as a permanent touchstone left by Daddy

2008

Table of Contents

Mary's Note ix

Notes on Glenn

The Music Man - *Howard Dyck* xi

The Poet - *Evelyn Dunsmore* xiii

The Spiritual Physician - *Rev. Dr. John Ambrose* xv

Editors' Note xvi

I 2007

  Poetry

      Maundy Thursday 3

      Job 5

      huron prayer 6

      Is it just the coffee? 7

  Prose

      Health Up-Dates 11

      A Speech for my family 25

      An Open Letter to Kapellmeister Bloss 28

II 2008

  Poetry

      My brother...35

  Prose

      Health Up-Dates 41

      What About Joseph?..61

III 2009

  Poetry

      January 20, 2009 67

      Breakfasts 69

It could be anywhere 71

Reading 73

The flower 75

Lois 76

MR. A's PLAYERS...78

Defining..79

Easter People 80

Mr. Bentley 82

O vos omnes 85

The Cove 88

Fairy Troll...90

How to Say 92

Snowy Song Sonnet 95

S'another Song sort'of Sonnet 96

Motherf*er 97

In the corner 99

Poetic ideas come and float................................101

In the Tube (or M.y R.ecurrent I.maginings) 103

I think I'll write a new poem 104

TDTTDD 105

Dappled Day's End 108

Some words are not for poetry – a set of 3 poems............111

Bag-of-bones 117

Mary Oliver Set

    Thirteenth Moon 123

    A Fourteenth Moon 125

    Dream Moon 127

Of Importance 129

My Camera 132

Au Revoir Aubade 134

Girl with the flower 135

Kris poems (a set of 3 poems for Maggie and Howard)

    Child of God..143

    She is your daughter 145

Into the woods 147

Old poems sit 149

Gone is my boyhood 150

Bloody Hell 151

Sonnet's Sonnet 153

Rhyming Resolution 154

He spat into dry ground 155

I am Keats as you are 159

Let's start at the top 163

Autumn's Glance 165

Daily Haikus 167

Glenn's Unfinished Symphony:

    That makes us dream...177

Fragments 186

Prose

    Health Up-Dates 193

IV B.C. 2006 and earlier

Poetry

    Credo..229

    my God is 231

    jp2 232

    The Day..233

    Indelible Ink..235

    L.A. 237

    Terrorism's Terror..238

    Hai..239

    Stress 240

    Gin's Tonic..241

    Buxtehude's Blues 242

    Coffee's Brews 243

    Katrina's Coup..244

    Silly Late Evening Evolving Poem..................................245

Jesus loves – this I know 246

Claudia of Cherubic Grace..248

When forty winters besiege thy brow 249

Auntie Meg 250

Katerjina 253

Prose

Moose Factory 257

Newcastle-on-Tyne—London 263

France 273

Kenya...280

A Mother's Note..293

About the author 297

Mary's Note:

Glenn Peirson, M.D., C.C.F.P.
July 22, 1965 - November 10, 2009

I first met my husband Glenn when I was a new resident at McMaster University Medical School in 1990. Glenn and I had been assigned to the same family practice unit. He apparently took notice of me, so the story goes, because in the pocket of my lab coat along with my stethoscope, pager and notebooks, was a slim, tattered volume of poems by Percy Bysshe Shelley. At the time I was reading the romantic poets as an antidote to the daily academic pressures and the long, late nights of call.

Little did I realize that Glenn was nurturing a deep and abiding love of poetry that would one day be his lasting legacy. Glenn was never one to venture into his areas of interest lightly. He was passionate and deeply committed to his pursuits whether it was his medical career, his family, his music or, of course, his poetry.

For years he principally read poetry and rarely wrote. He wished to know and understand the oeuvre. He read widely and formed deep attachments to certain poets – John Donne, John Keats, Gerard Manley Hopkins, Walt Whitman, Dylan Thomas, Mary Oliver, and Denise Levertov were among his favourites.

He did write some poetry in the early years of our married life (and before I knew him) – often to mark important milestones or as gifts to friends. However, he still considered himself an amateur as he furthered his reading and study of poetry. In the early years of the new millennium I gave him a book called "In the Palm of Your Hand" which was a textbook of sorts on poetry. It delved into the technical details of forms of poetry. Glenn loved this book – the esoterica of the minor forms fascinated him (an aubade anyone?).

Early in 2007 he was diagnosed with sinus cancer. As he began the long and torturous road of treatment and more treatment, he drew greater and greater comfort from reading and now writing poetry. Because he could not work, and was often confined to hospital or home, his considerable mental and spiritual energies were directed to writing poetry. While some of his work reflected on his cancer journey (Bag-of-bones), suffering (Job) and the transience of life (I am Keats as you are), much of his poetry at this time reflected on the beauty of our world (Dappled Days End), the small graces in everyday life (Is it just the coffee?) and souls who touched him (My Brother, Mr. Bentley). He found solace in music (That makes us dream - *unfinished*) and his steadfast Christian faith (O vos omnes). Despite his illness, his sense of humour was undiminished (Of Importance). Keeping the boredom of illness at bay, he found intellectual challenges in the technical aspects of poetry (Poetic Ideas Come and Float). He enjoyed the discipline of his daily Haiku and found consolation in his ongoing exploration of the sonnet form (Snowy Song Sonnet, Sonnet's Sonnet).

I hope that by experiencing this canon, the reader will get some sense of the man. In choosing to name this volume "I am Keats as you are," I acknowledge it was not lost on Glenn that he was like Keats – a young poet of great passions and loves snatched from us by illness at an all too early age.

Mary Claire Peirson
August 9, 2010

The Music Man:

On October 5, 2009, Glenn wrote in one of the last of his many inspired and inspiring emails which I and many others received from him,

> *"If I could negotiate my survival, I would not (yes, honestly) give up the cancer experience. Though, I have had enough of it now (vast understatement), and definitely do not recommend it to others!"*

He concluded that memo with these words which are imbued with the optimism, the fortitude and the boundless faith which always defined this remarkable father, husband, brother, son, colleague and friend,

> *"We are always open to your questions, concerns, gestures and good-will. We are, as always, allergic to pity and despair. We are blessed by family in all its iterations and thank you for all you are to us.*
> *Love, Glenn et al."*

Where do I begin in trying to sum up my friend Glenn Peirson? He was a rare one, was Glenn, a perfect blend of saint, clown, philosopher, pixie, artist, scholar. All of us who were privileged to know him are immeasurably richer for having walked with him. Glenn had a very big brain and an even bigger heart. He was funny, smart, profoundly spiritual, and highly literate. He was a genuine Renaissance man. He was Glenn and he was as true and loyal and intense a friend as anyone could ever hope to have. We experienced that in our family just very recently. Our daughter had quite suddenly taken critically ill and for a number of days her very survival hung in the balance. Disregarding his own ravaged condition, Glenn came to the hospital, and, in a most touching manner, asked the staff about her condition and the treatment she was being given. He then proceeded to comfort us. After that he went home and wrote a beautiful, eloquent, heart-felt set of poems, Kris poems (a set of 3 poems for Maggie and Howard) which Kristine and all of us in our family will treasure as long as we live. And he put together a compilation CD of many carefully-selected excerpts from the works of Bach...choral, organ, solo instrument, keyboard, even something sung by Bobby McFerrin. Glenn gave it a title - "For H&M (Howard and Maggie) B-A-C-H: Belief, Affirmation, Care, Healing". Over the years we have received many gifts of books and recordings from Glenn and Mary. This last one from the hand of a friend who knew that his own days were numbered is especially precious because it gave us strength and sustenance and courage and serenity during a very difficult time.

It was Robert Schumann who said that heaven gave us music so that the soul could beautify itself. Glenn Peirson's soul was indeed beautiful. He nourished it with the love of his family and friends, with his deep and abiding faith, and with the finest music that our civilization has been able to muster. His life was itself a symphony of grace, passion, love and generosity. The reverberations of that sublime music will be with us for a very long time.

Johann Sebastian Bach's towering St. John Passion concludes with a chorale which in its majesty and searing insight transcends time and space. The words are a fitting way to say "Auf Wiedersehen" (till we meet again) to our friend. We mourn his loss, and we celebrate his altogether remarkable life.

> *"O Lord, let your dearest angels*
> *At the final end carry my soul*
> *To the bosom of Abraham;*
> *Let the body in its chamber*
> *Meekly, without pain or suffering*
> *Rest until the judgment day.*
> *Then awaken me from death*
> *That my eyes will see you*
> *In all joy, O Son of God,*
> *My saviour and my mercy throne.*
> *Lord Jesus Christ, hear me,*
> *I will praise you for all eternity."*

Howard Dyck
November, 2009

The Poet:

on: *That makes us dream:*

Seeking all his life to articulate and celebrate the abundant manifestations of God in our human lives, Glenn reveals much about his love of his fellow sojourners in "That Makes us Dream" as he explores his soul's journey through music towards an understanding of eternity.

I love how, after his thesis in the first stanza, he opens with an invitation for us to "Sit on the edge of my futon / in the dark / and listen", which paves the way for the sharing of his thoughts throughout the poem. We are participants in his passion even if we (read "I") lack his deep knowing of the works he cites. And in that second stanza, too, he reveals the depth of his passion: "... is it possible not to pray when / immersed in this sound world?" and we learn more about him, the poet and the man. And then he leads us, comradely, back into his life, into the beginnings of his immersion into music as we share with him Bach's "Dona nobis pacem" in his "1970s panelled basement bedroom" - and so, forward through time, and the musical moments which fill his soul and "catch the heart off guard and blow it open," (Heaney) often weeping in ecstasy.

And to the near past in which the ecstasy of music is so healing that it is "emptying [our] hearts / of any misgiving in life" and transporting [us] / freed of any medical tether, tenuous bond of mortality", thus preparing us, the sharers, for the absolute of music in all things mundane – as well as preparing us for eternity. And sharing in the almost-anguish of "Sander's Reproaches", only to be raised up again in the assurance of justness and rightness: "Lord, You have done nothing / You have not offended."

And on to the future, reflected in the present, when his daughter "plays his Little prelude in E minor" and we are there too to witness "the communication of sheer beauty" in her love of Bach.

It is as if this glimpse of the future catapults him, the poet and the man, again into the past from his singing of "Allegri's treble" (and is there a more divine piece of music on the planet than the "Miserere"?), to "Beatlemania" and then he pulls us helter-skelter - and there is an urgency in the reminiscences here - to those venues which were the gateways to allow him to feel, sing, articulate his passion and to connect him with his "companions Bede and Cuthbert" and later his "musician son" ("quirky in-his-own-world"): Ely Cathedral, the Chapel of King's College, Durham Cathedral, Westminster Cathedral and the Abbey, St. Martin in-the-Fields.

And so to return to his thesis through the primary focal point of his passion - Bach - and to conclude that "light comes through a path connected to darkness / darkness is never avoided / in fact, Bach will always explore darkness / sadness, grief, loss, waywardness / In this he connects us to every human being / and then elevates our sorrow and despair / through music of the most utter beauty." As he makes this soul-centred discovery, we are there too, as he has invited us to be all along, in "the sound [that] goes out / ...comes back eventually and surrounds you / enfolds and bathes you with its / ambient richness." We are partners in this journey of discovery because the man and the poet have asked us to be. And it's a bit like voyeurism, except that we are so deeply grateful for having been invited to glimpse into the soul of a good and great man. This shared journey transports us, too, "beyond the mere "participation in music / to the ephemeral." And what shared sadness, yet what exaltation in the knowledge that "there is no conclusion, denouement" in Bach's "Kunst der Fuge" except to know that the "mysterious final fugue" - like the poet/man's life "is left floating away like a balloon" into the certainty of eternity.

I thank him for this companionship, for his friendly, loving arm across my shoulder, for his confidence in me, the reader, for his love.

Evelyn Dunsmore
June, 2010

The Spiritual Physician

Friendships often begin inauspiciously. I first met Glenn Peirson at a small gathering of church people seeking some guidance on planning for their future. Glenn attended the meeting as co-chair of the congregation's Ministry and Personnel Committee. I had come as a volunteer consultant. As I learned that night, communication with Glenn was always easy and always invigorating.

Circumstances over the following months led to my accepting an invitation to become the interim minister of the congregation. Glenn, who was a little more than half my age, suddenly became my 'boss'. What a joy! What a privilege!

Through many conversations by phone, in person, and through e-mails, the association blossomed into a friendship. Chats that should have focused on personnel issues wandered off to favourite choral and instrumental works, the future of the church, much-loved poetry, the meaning behind ambiguous passages of scripture, favourite foods, and on and on.

How I treasured those chats, knowing that I was only one among many receiving the spiritual and intellectual largesse of this man; and knowing also the deep struggle he was having with the advancing cancer.

He honoured me at one point, by sharing a selection of his poems. I sat for a full evening, reading them over and over, at times shedding tears at their beauty and directness. One, entitled 'Jesus loves - this I know' (October 7, 2005), lies carefully folded in my wallet. It has become a mantra of hope.

Thankfully, Glenn's gift of poetry, coming from a life and faith so fully lived, will now be available to a wider audience.

The Reverend Dr. John Ambrose

Editors' Note

Glenn was a man blessed with abundant intellect, compassion, insight, musical and literary talent, and extraordinary humour. His death was a great loss to his family, friends, spiritual and musical communities, local community and his patients.

When Glenn was taken hostage by cancer for a three year journey, he explained very early that this was his "solitary journey." He suffered greatly in his physical, emotional and social life. He did not suffer spiritually, as this volume of poetry and writings demonstrates.

His most abiding legacy was what he had written. Ironically, his illness provided the time, context and motivation to more fully explore his poetic and prosaic expression. In preparing this book, we scoured three computers for files, found journals, sorted through old letters and had deciphering marathons on some of his *oh-he-sure-was-a-doctor* handwriting.

After undertaking the daunting task of sifting and ordering, we concluded that his poetry and prose of 2007, 2008 and 2009 must come first as it represents the largest body of work and addresses his final and extraordinary three year journey.

Thus, this book progresses through the "solitary journey" years first. Poetry introduces each section, and the prose of each year follows the year's poetry. Then comes the second section, the B.C. (Before Cancer) section, similarly ordered.

Shortly after Glenn's death, November 10, 2009, an endowment fund was established to honour Glenn's love of music. The Dr. Glenn D. Peirson Fund for the Arts – *supporting the musical arts in our community* – granted its first award to the Guelph Youth Singers in Spring, 2010.

To learn more about Glenn and the Fund: www.physicianmusician.com

Poetry is about beauty, pure and complicated
the unfolding of a flower
the rebirth of a dormant idea
the retelling of tragedy to Shakespearean intent
the revealing of personal scars which give access to the ineffable

from ***Some words are not for poetry I***

Mary Peirson and Ellyn Peirson

I

Poetry 2007

April 5, 2005: Maundy Thursday

(February 8, 2009 and before)

"This bread I break was once the oat"
was once my Maundy Thursday
was once my body before the break.

"The great wonder," she writes,
"is that the human cells of His flesh and bone
didn't explode"
and I wondered, that Thursday,
as I observed the clear fluid
trickling down the tubing
into me,
would those inhuman cells explode?

"The *onening* …" she writes,
"opened Him utterly
to the pain of all minds, all bodies"
the onening for me,
of my cup of poison,
my salvation,
opening me to newness?

Innocuous dripping, clear fluid with
sinister intent,
circumcision of non-self, cell by cell,
breaking bread, oat by oat.

Clear mix into plasma, red diffusion by
necessary toxin,
a vein of despondency, temporary brokenness
letting health bleed forth.

"This flesh you break, this blood you let
Make desolation in the vein," he writes,
the bread real, the wine feels ripe

when spilled or rather split
by human condition,
mortal technique, with
divine aspiration.

This bread I break, Dylan Thomas 19
On a Theme from Julian's Chapter XXI, Denise Levertov 1987

JOB
(started July 12, 2007)

And the Lord bereaved Job of all his hair, and then shriveled his body so that he was devoid of strength: and Job said very little.

This was after the Lord had taunted Job with disfigurement and mutilation of his face. Then the Lord God added fire to the torments of Job. His bones were poisoned and then his skin lit to flame. And Job could not swallow, nor eat, and his weakness grew.

The Lord saw that Job was suffering greatly, but this did not suffice: it did not suffice that Job was anemic, leukopenic, in renal failure, profoundly paresthetic in hands and feet. Job's nasal passageways did dry up and occlude, and his breathing was laboured. Job's eye crusted and wept. Job wretched because he could not swallow, and he vomited hideously as there was no food in his stomach.

The Lord God made Job withdraw from his family and his life. He was lashed to his bed all hours of the day. And Job simply existed; he had nothing else to do.

And Job did lament, but not against God. He lamented for his old self, his family, his responsibilities, his dreams. And Job wept bitterly, but not against God: For who else would be his redeemer? For who else was his creator? Who else could save Job from his plight?

So Job prayed through the anguish and remained faithful to the Lord God, waiting an answer to his prayer. Job did not speak, for he had lost this ability as well.

And the Lord waited patiently also.

huron prayer
(September 3, 2007)

blue huron healer
the birch suckers sap power
lop them – one-one-one

Is it just the coffee?
(November 2007)

Is it just the coffee?
carefully organized, procured, chosen
lovingly, regularly, determinedly roasted
milled, not ground, dark or light
       or somewhere between
machine of choice – device du jour
your time and expertise (primarily to my benefit …
       or at least demands)

Patiently waiting while I took
       my hiatus from the
       venerable bean (amongst
       other things)
You forewent the ritual of the bean
       and waited
lovingly, regularly, determinedly
       you waited
       and waited

Now back to the glorious bean,
       I am not ravenous, but
       more deeply appreciative of
       its chocolate tones, warmth,
       layers of flavour, mouth-
       coating properties, and pick-me-
       up-relax ritual

I am more than appreciative
       of your coffee
       of you
I cherish you
       and the coffee you so
       lovingly make for me

every day
    twice

When I am away from you
    (your coffee)
I lose some balance, some
    vigor (some caffeine)

You are my beloved, this I
    know more than ever
and I do love you more than
    coffee

but it is good (your coffee),
    terribly good.

Prose: 2007

Date: March 26, 2007
Subject: health update

Dear friends,

It has been a few weeks since I sent you our news of my sinus cancer. We have been busy, and obviously anxious since then. But we have received such an outpouring of support, prayer, and concern that we are overwhelmed by the true meaning of friendship. Again, we apologize for our inability to respond individually, but between organizing our work and family lives, and attending medical appointments, we have little free time (perhaps this is good right now).

I have some good and bad news to share with you.

First, the surgical date is set for April 3, which at times seems very close for us, and at other times far too remote. We have the utmost confidence in our surgeons and really feel we are in the right place for treatment!

Next, some not-so-good news ... Dr. Y. called me on Thursday because of concerns with my MRI, which had been further reviewed by radiology experts. The tumour is quite large and has compromised the area of my right eye. My eye will have to be removed as part of the surgery. To be perfectly honest, I was prepared for this and felt that the loss of my eye was quite probable. Mary and I are really quite OK with this information. It is the size and extent of the tumour that gives us stress. We are very focused on getting the surgery done and being on the treatment path.

I know this information may be upsetting to you, but we would rather you understood what is happening, so we don't feel the burden of sharing information after the fact. We (or at least I) still have a sense of humour ... I'm sure there are possibilities for designer prostheses ... perhaps seasonal variations, declarations of mood, who knows? This will not change my ability to work or drive or drive my family crazy with incessant teasing and corny jokes.

We have met the rest of the cancer team and have an excellent understanding of what is to come with radiation and chemotherapy, which starts in combination

6 weeks post-operatively. I have received tremendous support from my staff, my colleagues, and the medical community in Cambridge. My concerns about my practice have been alleviated.

Lastly, some fun news. I decided to ask the surgical team on Friday what they thought my chances were for participating in the May 5 Tactus Shakespeare concert that I have been heavily involved in creating. We talked about my music and post-op recovery, and they said that my chances of singing were decent, that the concert should be one of my recuperation goals! So, I can't guarantee my involvement, but I shall endeavour to give it a go, perhaps looking a bit like an Elizabethan torture victim, but that should just enhance the drama of the evening.

Your support, good wishes, prayers are all deeply appreciate by me, Mary, Theo and Henry, and our family at large. It will really not be possible to have visitors in hospital, so come to the May 5 concert (www.tactusvocalensemble.com ... tickets will be available through the RiverRun Centre soon). I believe we are doing well under the circumstances. We push ahead with a positive outlook, tempered by moments of uncertainty, but always grounded in our faith and its comforts.

We will keep you posted,
Glenn

Date: April 17, 2007
Subject: next health update

Hello again friends,

I need to let you know my current state of affairs once again, as our roller-coaster ride took another turn from my last email, but we are now on the "road to cure" and much relieved to have the treatment underway.

My surgery for definitive biopsy was 2 weeks ago today. The surgery was minimally invasive and finally gave a specific answer to the type of cancer - it is the most common type for this extremely rare malignancy. I was kept in London to see the oncology team the next morning. We were expecting to begin preparation for radiation with some chemo, but instead were advised to start intensive chemotherapy alone.

So, much to our unpreparedness (we've become imminently flexible though), we plunged into a different therapy path. I stayed in London through to Easter morning, received my course of toxins, and was sent home with 2 days left on the final infusion with a intravenous access stationed in my upper arm - this will stay in place as long as needed, and should allow me to get the majority of chemo treatment at home, with a minimum of hospitalization. It was a rather extraordinary Holy Week, but led to a tremendous reduction in Mary's and my anxiety.

Last week proved that chemotherapy is, indeed, not a walk in the park! I won't go into detail, except to say that it ain't pretty, ain't fun, and ain't like anything you've ever been through before (unless you've had chemo). Almost made a deal with God in the wee hours of last Thursday, and that just ain't me!!

The good news is, my facial swelling has decreased dramatically, my wife still loves me despite my torrid affair with all manner of porcelain appliances last week, and I've actually feel great the past couple of days. In fact, I likely feel better now than I have for many months ... this is encouraging. Oh, yes, my children still profess deep, abiding, and wonderfully naive love for me, even if I will be profoundly bald in a matter of days.

The plan is 2 more sessions of this chemo routine (on weeks 4 & 7 ... i.e. resuming next Wed.), about 3 weeks later followed by 7 weeks of M-F radiation treatments with weekly chemo, all in London. This will take us to mid-July or so. Surgery, if needed, could occur as early as 4 weeks after that. But, we are living on a day-to-day basis, not looking too far ahead, and embracing the small yet significant victories thus far. It is clear to me that this is, indeed, a battle. The medical poison is directly fighting the abnormal non-me cells, with some casualties to normal cells that can't get out of the way (i.e. side-effects!).

All-in-all we are doing well as a family. Theo and Henry seem as normal as they ever could be. Mary has more strength of character than I ever cared to know! And my extended family has been supportive beyond measure.

Thank you again for your best wishes, support and prayers. Please don't feel obligated to respond!

Glenn

consider:
1. donating blood with Canadian Blood Services www.bloodservices.ca
2. purchasing a ticket to Shakespeare's Music: A Day in the Life of Will *on Saturday May 5 at 8:00 p.m. at the Guelph Youth Music Centre www.tactusvocalensemble.com ... tickets through the River Run Centre*

Hello once again,

This email brings some significant good news and a plea for your help! I am finished 2 rounds of chemotherapy, and though the chemo is quite a bit less than fun, my facial swelling has reduced to almost insignificant. Before my surgery my right eye was partially swollen shut and the swelling was quite dramatic. The medical team in London seems most encouraged and surprised by the obvious radical reduction in tumour size. The chemo is not intended to be curative, but the reduction in swelling is most welcome, has led me to be pain free (at least in my face), and outweighs the more unsavoury effects of the poison.

The radiation treatment has been planned out and will start in early June. This is treatment with curative intent. It will be an intense time of daily travel to London over 7 weeks, but most treatments last about 15 minutes, so the actual time in London will be brief. I mentioned to Mary yesterday that luckily London holds no other history, affection, or purpose in our lives, so my growing feelings of detesting the place can be what they are without any worry of tainting the city for any other reason! This is not to say that I am not deeply appreciative of the superb care I have been getting and will continue to receive. I will simply be happy not to visit the city again at some point in my long-lived existence.

I was able to travel into Cambridge on Tuesday and take my (wonderful) staff out for lunch. The weather was glorious and the food tasted pretty decent, especially after my recumbent week. I had just enough energy on Saturday to sing with Tactus in our most excellent Shakespeare concert - part of my "kicking cancer in the lower orifice" approach to things, most gratifying. Mary, Theo and Henry are doing extremely well, and since I will be sidelined for Old Vic's birthday weekend, we will pull the kids from school next Monday and make our own long weekend as we open up the beloved cottage. Our cottage quickly became a sanctuary in our lives, and obviously this will be even more so this summer, as we will spend as much time there as my treatment and recovery will allow. Perhaps swimming in the crystal clear waters of Lake Huron will be the most healing experience of all.

May 26th brings the season-ending concert at the River Run Centre for Theo and Henry and the Guelph Youth Singers. Tactus will be making a cameo appearance, which was arranged some time ago. This now takes on greater significance, as the timing should work for me to join in and share the stage with my kids. As much as we all love and adore Mary, her best place will be in the audience that night (respectfully submitted xoxo).

Lastly and most importantly, my sister-in-law Sara has organized a Peirson-Beingessner team for the Canadian Cancer Society "Relay for Life", which is an annual fundraiser which takes place in many communities across the country. Teams are formed around a cancer survivor (prematurely moi for our 'Team Cure') and participate in a 7:00 p.m. to 7:00 a.m. continuous relay walk. The Guelph event is slated for Friday June 15 at Guelph Lake and the 13 member Team Cure will pitch our tents and hoof ourselves around the track during this time.

Please consider donating through this worthy fundraiser to the Canadian Cancer Society. Donations over $20 are tax deductible. The simplest method of donation is through our web portals. Please give generously. The lifetime incidence of Cancer in Canada is somewhere between 30 - 50%, which is staggering. We are all touched by this disease and there are few more worthy recipients for donation than the CCS. If you have already been contacted about this by another family member, feel free to donate through them. Another opportunity through the website is to purchase luminaries. These are candles set up around the track which are lit as dusk settles on the relay. Each luminary is purchased (for $5) in honour of someone affected by cancer. Apparently this is quite a moving ceremony at the event, and provides a tangible symbol in addition to a donation. Each team member has a web portal for pledges. Our object as a team is to widen the circle of donors and maximize the pledges! Please feel free to pass on our links to anyone who might be interested in donating.

Again, many thanks for your support, prayers, and concerns.

Glenn

Date: July 9, 2007
Subject: a brief health update

Dear friends,

It has been a little while since I updated you on the treatment saga. I will be brief, as last week was extremely long and exhausting. Needless to say, the cancer treatment itself continues to go very well ... the side-effects, not so well (no shock here). I don't mean to belabor you with details, but I am aware that I need you to understand where we are at present.

I told someone recently that getting chemo is a bit like putting something up on a bulletin board with a sledge hammer - it works well, but leaves some collateral damage. That was before I was introduced to the full effects of radiation while taking chemo - here the bulletin board item is further treated with a flame thrower just to be sure!

The long weekend was a real low point for me and us, as my swallowing dysfunction got profoundly worse and I had great difficulty with fluids let alone food. By the time we got home on Monday, we knew that it was time for a radical change of plan, and so we prepared for me to be admitted to hospital in London on Tuesday. They treated my dehydration and scheduled me for a gastric feeding tube, which was thankfully inserted on Thursday. With good behaviour, I coerced the powers that be into letting me come home Friday night.

So I am now fed and hydrated through the feeding tube, and can attempt to eat and drink by mouth as much as possible. This should help my 179 lb. frame get back into the necessary shape for healing. There are 2 weeks of radiation left, further chemo is up in the air, and I am currently hooked up to the feeding pump virtually 24 hours per day (this should reduce to about 18 hours soon). Mary and I feel a great amount of relief to know that my body is more stable, but it was a most challenging and unpleasant week or two. Fatigue continues, but hey, what's new?

Theo and Henry are extremely well. Theo turns 10 this week while away at Camp Ganadaoweh, and Henry hits his beloved operetta camp tomorrow. We continue to feel extremely supported, but are really limited at present in our ability to respond adequately to well-wishers by email, phone, or in person, as my days in London are long, and we are simply tired. Our spirits are strong, our outlook positive, our bold expectation for healing ongoing.

I will try to write again sooner, but desperately look forward to finishing the radiation and having some real recuperation time.

Again, many thanks for your support, prayers, and interest in our journey!

Love,
Glenn

PS. Our TEAM CURE collected more than $22,000 in donations in the Canadian Cancer Society Relay for Life in June. The Guelph event raised over $80,000 with 30 teams in its first year, so TEAM CURE certainly led the way. Many, many thanks to all of you who generously supported the cause! I would like to thank people individually, but this could take quite some time. Look out for TEAM CURE again next year, as this is one event worthy of reinvestment.

Date: September 17, 2007
Subject: health update

Dear friends,

Last time I wrote I apologized for the length of time since previously writing. And now I've waited even longer - chalk that up to some significant time up at our cottage recuperating and the busyness of getting our kids back to school.

My chemo and radiation treatments finished the end of July and, as promised, I felt worse over the next couple of weeks. I had a transfusion up at picturesque Lion's Head Hospital, thanks to a good friend who has practiced there ever since we worked there in residency, and 2 days later had a major turn around, began eating by mouth, and within days had stopped using the feeding tube entirely. Really this change felt like the transformation from spectator in life to participant again.

We saw my oncologist later in August and received a good report. Now I am awaiting seeing the surgeon next week and hopefully his formal pronouncement that I am clear of disease and finished treatment. This is our fervent prayer, expectation, and hope. The surgeon did tell me in July that he felt my need for surgery was near "nil", but hearing it a final time will be most gratifying. It will also make all the suffering worthwhile!

My major issues at present are fatigue and weakness. My weight is steady, but still down about 25 lbs. (I am not exactly Charles Atlas these days). Mary and I plan to slowly tackle my exercise tolerance and get some beef on these bones. My oncologist has said that my hope to return to work part-time in November is realistic, which should prevent me from having my staff divorce me.

Theo and Henry are back in action at school and in their extracurriculars. I was well enough to see Cirque du Soleil's new Kooza show in Toronto with the kids in August - a magnificent show and magical experience for me. Our cottage has been a real sanctuary for us and home doesn't feel like a prison anymore, as my ability to move about, bother Mary, tease the children, do dishes and laundry has normalized.

I will send an update after seeing the surgeon, then hope not to need to bother you folks so much with the trivialities of our humble little life!

Glenn

Dear friends,

Please forgive my lack of brevity with this (final) communication. The news is all good at this juncture, and I want to share the details with you – it's the least you deserve after reading all my other emails!

> **from <u>The Magician's Nephew</u> by C.S. Lewis,
> Chapters 12, 14, 15**
>
> *"I asked, are you ready?" said the Lion.*
>
> *"Yes," said Digory. He had for a second some wild idea of saying "I'll try to help you if you'll promise to help about my mother," but he realised in time that the Lion was not at all the sort of person one could try to make bargains with. But when he had said "Yes," he thought of his mother, and he thought of the great hopes he had had, and how they were all dying away, and a lump came in his throat and tears in his eyes, and he blurted out: "But please, please – won't you – can't you give me something that will cure Mother?" Up till then he had been looking at the Lion's great feet and the huge claws on them; now, in his despair, he looked up at its face. What he saw surprised him as much as anything in his whole life. For the tawny face was bent down near his own and (wonder of wonders) great shining tears stood in the Lion's eyes. They were such big, bright tears compared with Digory's own that for a moment he felt as if the Lion must really be sorrier about his mother than he was himself.*
>
> *"My son, my son," said Aslan. "I know. Grief is great ..."*

Mary and I, Theo and Henry have been through the most difficult time in our lives over the past 6 months. Our anxiety at times was almost unbearable. The constant sense of my mortality was real in a way one cannot imagine if not actually experienced. There was a phase when Mary and I did not talk of anything beyond the next 12 hours, as we stopped looking ahead in any fashion, stopped dreaming and imagining our lives, which has always been such a strong feature of our relationship. Yet Theo and Henry were always, always able to 'go with the flow' – to respect me (and Mary) when the suffering was great and to deeply connect with us when the moments were lighter and softer (often simply time on our bed watching a program together). They are marvelous and grounding creatures, filled with real and unadulterated love.

Whether you have a faith or not, you know that our little family of Peirsons has a Faith that emanates from the core of who we are as created beings. I never felt fearful of death. I never railed at God about my circumstances (really not part of my belief system). I did, however, feel great fear about losing my family, about not watching my children grow and develop over the years. Almost a selfish instinct, I couldn't get my head around the idea of not being with them, shaping and being shaped by them. This tortured me when I let it. I really found no conciliation in any idea of nirvana beyond this.

And I felt trapped in my withering body, heading off to London for my daily torture. Against these fears, death seemed a probable preference to more treatment … and yet, you just do it. Going through cancer, its physical and emotional torments, its horrible treatments, is not heroism. It is simply something you go through. Many people of all walks and sizes go through it. One musters one's resources, and goes through it, bit by bit.

"… And the Witch tempted you to do another thing, my son, did she not?"

"Yes, Aslan. She wanted me to take an apple home to Mother."

"Understand, then, that it would have healed her; but not to your joy or hers. The day would have come when both you and she would have looked back and said it would have been better to die in that illness."

And Digory could say nothing, for tears choked him and he gave up all hopes of saving his mother's life; but at the same time he knew that the Lion knew what would have happened, and that there might be things more terrible even than losing someone you love by death. But now Aslan was speaking again, almost in a whisper: "That is what would have happened, child, with a stolen apple. It is not what will happen now. What I give you now will bring joy. It will not, in your world, give endless life, but it will heal. Go. Pluck her an apple from the Tree."

So, we saw the surgeon at the end of September, he of always bad or worsening news, and he was almost giddy (for him) about the CT scan and his examination of me. "I wouldn't believe it if I hadn't seen it with my own eyes," was what he said. I asked him what he thought in pondering the surgical plans from last March. "Thank God we didn't do surgery," he replied!

We saw the oncologists in early October, and they both declared me in **remission**, with no evidence of tumour on the scan. The chemo oncologist has signed off, with plenty of advice for all my smouldering chemo side-effects. The radiation oncologist will see me again in January, and sees good healing from all the nasty radiation effects.

My eye is fine, aside from issues of dryness and irritation. I will develop a cataract on the right side, but c'est la vie – a privilege, in retrospect! I have almost no saliva, which is actually a big problem, but will hopefully improve over months. Everything takes months – my hand and foot numbness, my bald patches, my eyelashes, my congestion, my facial swelling, my anemia and kidney function, my fatigue and skinniness (we've hired a trainer to help put some muscle back on). Every day I build a little more strength and have a little more facial stubble. I do many of life's ordinary tasks with joy, and Mary and I feel relatively stress-free. Hey, compared to having a life-threatening illness, there's little that can stress us right now.

I see the surgeon again in December with a CT scan beforehand, and have an MRI pending. I will be in surveillance for years, but this is where we prayed I would be and we are so filled with thanks for arriving in mostly one piece. "Cure" is a label generally given after 5 years of being cancer-free.

Remission is where I am, gladly so.
I start back to work part-time in November, and look forward to more normalcy with that. My office has run extremely well without me (with many thanks to my staff and colleagues), but it will be good to be able to tease my staff on a regular basis again (no, I don't just tease my children).

You, my friends, have been remarkable with Mary and me in oh so many ways. We thank you for your deep and earnest and ongoing prayers, your support and good wishes, for your little distractions, and for your food. I have never felt such support in my life, and I hope I never require such support again!! It has been a very humbling path. Cancer is sadly ubiquitous, touches us all at some point, and transforms life, sometimes with healing and sometimes with death.

> *And there she lay as he had seen her lie so many other times, propped up on the pillows, with a thin, pale face that would make you cry to look at. Digory took the Apple of Life out of his pocket...*

> *The brightness of the Apple threw strange lights on the ceiling. Nothing else was worth looking at: you couldn't look at anything else. And the smell of the Apple of Youth was as if there was a window in the room that opened on Heaven ...*

> *He peeled it and cut it up and gave it to her piece by piece. And no sooner had she finished it than she smiled and her head sank back on the pillow and she was asleep: a real, natural, gentle sleep, without any of those nasty drugs, which was, as Digory knew, the thing in the whole world that she wanted most. And he was sure now that her face looked a little different. He bent down and kissed her very softly and stole out of the room with a beating heart; taking the core of the Apple with him. For the rest of the day, whenever he looked at things about him, and saw how ordinary and unmagical they were, he hardly dared to hope; but when he remembered the face of Aslan he did hope.*

Life is a gift at all times. Life is a gift at its entrance and continuance and exit. My outcome, my remission, my revocation of tumour is a gift of life. I do not wear this lightly, and go forward with immense gratitude.

Glenn

A Speech for my family
November 2, 2007

I present to you, my family, the frightening prospect that I have actually written a speech for our get-together this evening!

(pause – time for wailing and gnashing of teeth)

The obvious reason for this is that I have too much time on my hands, not enough projects, and need to return to work.

Or, perhaps the obvious reason is that I want to formally and explicitly convey my deep gratitude to all of you for what you have offered me and us over this past 6 months of trial and tribulation.

There are two risks in approaching this idea for a speech. The first is simply not to follow-through and do it – not to avail myself of this perfect opportunity. I've been wanting to send out a thank-you email for a few weeks now for the "Gong Show" event, but an email didn't feel right. And then the plans for our Relay for Life dinner at Artisanale came together and here we are without the distraction of the next generation (bless their little souls!).

It is too easy to leave so much communication these days to the written word. And spoken opportunities like this are so rare – perhaps an underprepared toast at a wedding, or an overprepared tribute at a funeral, or that last cue-card speech in Grade 8. We don't have need to speak to an audience very often, and to address two families, complete in their 16 members and with a singular attention, and without the speaker being father and mafia Don, well … we just don't make these speeches anymore.

The second risk? The emotional risk, the risk of "laying it on the line". I certainly don't care about speaking to you in a restaurant, where other unintended ears may hear; but there is a vulnerability in speaking candidly and with an open heart. As we all know, life is too short … too short to skip this chance of communication. Not to tell you how much I love you all is foolish. Not to speak this truth because of the risk of displaying emotion would be extremely short-sighted.

So, as you can see, I've written the damn speech!

Three months ago I was still fighting for my life and literally felt like hell. We were all collectively fighting for my life and did not, could not know what the outcome would be. I've written bits of this speech before, as part of my funeral or obituary. You would be amazed at how the mind entertains when under great duress! But here I am, a little creative of haircut, a little lighter of mass, a little uneven of shaving needs, and I don't want to wait until a funeral before expressing my feelings.

Our TEAM CURE Relay for Life success last June was a rather monumental experience for me – so positive and so good in its object. It was also just before the wheels fell off my wagon, and my summer of discontent, dysfunction, and disease began. I so look forward to the reinstitution of our team next June and promise to stay overnight with you this time!

I will not address each of you individually, as we would like to move onto dessert at some point, and I do not wish to compare in anyway what any of you have offered me and us. You have all offered us much, perhaps without realizing it at times: from the simplicity of love and deep concern, to the profundity of prayer, to your company, your good will, your kinship, to the openness whereby we could approach anyone in our family with a request and it would be given top priority response. It is not possible, even with a family smaller than ours, to apportion out the care needed over these months into equal slices of work. Needless to say, it is crystal clear that our family would offer any and all support imaginable to help us through this crisis.

We fervently hope that none of you needs such support in the future – but please know that it is there in abundance with your family.

I would like to highlight the most extraordinary person in my life: Mary, the one and only. She not only was my very strength, but did everything, literally. She was a single mother through the worst times, while nursing me continually and having all the worry on top of these duties. She is an extraordinary person, wife, and mother, and she deserves my highest praise and thanks. She even thought I had some semblance of looking good while she plastered my face with Glaxal cream, injected medication through my belly wall, and watched me wretch every evening before bed. She even shared my bed throughout this whole battle (and I mean "sharing bed" in the most innocent sense over this time).

And so we've come out the other side, with ongoing thanks to our Maker, and with a huge debt of gratitude to our family and many friends, colleagues, and even acquaintances. We are delighted that I am in remission and not unrealistic about the burden of surveillance (though a burden we gladly accept). We pray that this will stay behind us now, and we honestly look at becoming deeper, more caring, more appreciative individuals. We also pray that our own small and larger family will be positively shaped by this life-changing experience.

Your recent variety show, more than anything in particular, highlighted what a wonderful, creative, nicely crazy, loving bunch of people these two families are. This is rare stuff – just look around and find another two families that could possibly have put an evening of true fellowship together like that!

"That which doesn't kill us makes us stronger." Now, I am no fan of Nietzsche, but this rings true to me at present. I am, however, a great fan of Kierkegaard: "Life can only be understood backwards; but it must be lived forwards." It is very easy for Mary and me to look backwards right now, to ponder the wreckage, where everything imploded and yet we are somehow still walking away from it, shaking our heads in a certain disbelief. And yet it is where we are headed that compels us, that allows us to rebuild our dreams, that is our life.

"Love is all, it gives all, and it takes all," says Kierkegaard. And so it does and is. Love certainly sustained us and spurred us on. It was embodied in the work of illness and kept us steady throughout.

And finally (please keep your applause to a dull roar), our Faith has been the foundation for us, like a safety net that we could never fall through. It will take more time and reflection to put adequate words to the importance of this. Kierkegaard says, "Faith is the highest passion in a human being. Many in every generation may not come that far, but none comes further." We believe we cannot go further than where our Faith takes us, and what a journey it can be! We do not understand Faith; it is irrational by nature. Without this passion, though, I'm not sure we would have had the strength to negotiate the passage …

Thanks for listening!

An Open Letter to
Kapellmeister Bloss and the Dublin Senior Choir
November 6, 2007

Dear Michael and Choir,

I feel compelled to comment on your performance of the Faure Requiem this past Sunday. What a beautiful achievement for the choir; and so unexpected to have a full mass integrated (shocking) into the All Saints' service. I saw the opening movement of the Faure on the front page of the bulletin and was so pleased, as the music means much to me, and then opened the bulletin to see the whole shebang. I can even forgive the intentional misplacement of the Pie Jesu.

A certain Larry Sugden may recall, but I won't hold him to it, a young lad of I think 11 years finishing his treble career with Faure's Pie Jesu in the midst of a Requiem performance. My voice broke just weeks after that Lenten concert at St. George's, here in Guelph, some 30 years ago. Larry was just 18 at the time, by the way.

I don't think it a stretch to presume that Dublin was the only United church in our fair nation that had a full choral mass performed liturgically this past Sunday. I've sung and heard the Faure many times, always in concert. How wonderful to hear it in the context of a service, and so well performed. Kudos to the whole choir for excellent blend, intonation, and shaping of text. Praise to each section of the choir for its contribution to the overall sound and its very fine part-work. It would be remiss of me not to mention the tenors' dramatic "Hosanna" at the end of the Sanctus! Neil and Mary Lynne deserve special praise for their solo work as well.

Michael, your direction was incisive – such a good pace for a chamber performance like this. And your organ work was atmospheric and wonderfully French (especially for a Kapellmeister).

Two more points of reflection, if I may. Don't worry, you can get back to your practice at some point. (It's hard to push someone off his soapbox when he's not even present!)

On my first occasion being in London by myself, I arrived at Victoria Station with little idea where to begin and hours to kill before I was due at my accommodation. I attended vespers at Westminster Cathedral, then sauntered down to Westminster Abbey, where I found a concert posting for that evening (Palm Sunday) of the Allegri Miserere and Faure Requiem: the exact pairing of my final boy solo concert. I attended in the bliss that only jetlag can give, and was immersed in Faure's magnificent work in that great cathedral.

I was equally immersed this past Sunday, which brings me to my final point of communication. The worst of my illness this summer brought me to some different considerations with my life. I don't mind sharing with you that I, at times, pondered the programming of my own funeral, which will be (some decades hence!) structured around Faure's Requiem. I had kept this quiet until you startled me with your performance on Sunday. And so, with my movement into remission, I can embrace the All Saints' service and the most joyful Requiem in my life.

Thank you,
Glenn

Date: December 20, 2007
Subject: Wednesday

Dear friends,

As you all know, and I've asked Mum to forward this message to her prayer list, yesterday went well for us. The reason I contacted you earlier in the week was to request your prayer on an anxious day for Mary and me. I had (joyfully) received the label of remission back in September, but October's MRI report was conflicting this somewhat and we didn't have a real opportunity to discuss this until yesterday. We knew that the stakes were high if Dr. Y. recommended surgery to determine if there was any residual cancer.

He is a most serious character, but was clear and very positive that MRI report is just showing artifact from scar tissue (would have been nice to hear that 2 months ago!), the CT scan from last week was essentially normal (he said if he didn't know my history, it would look like a normal CT of the sinuses in someone with a cold), and that my response to treatment has been a "miracle".

Now, he also said that if my cancer were to recur, he doesn't think that surgery would be an option and that I would not survive that illness ... so, a little salt with the sugar. When we got back to the car, Mary looked at me earnestly and said "No more tumours, okay?" I am only going to eat flax seed and Vitamin D for the rest of my (long) life.

We are not stressed by this latter information and know that all cancers are bad news when they recur. If this were to happen, God forbid, we would still have hope and there are always treatment options and ... prayer!

It is important to us that you understand that I will not be entitled to wear that label "cured" until at least 5 years have passed. We still live under the shadow of cancer known as "remission," but we are not in any way controlled by this. Surveillance and a measure of uncertainty are normal for anyone with life-threatening cancer. Yesterday's news is cause for relief from some fears for us. This relief supersedes any celebration. We celebrated my remission in September when it was fresh, and we are simply grateful now that this has been restated and reinforced. We appreciate all your support, but please understand that yesterday's good news is not new news ... it's a reiteration of what we were told in September and reassurance that remission is my current destination.

Your ongoing prayers, though perhaps less focused than yesterday, do sustain us. The community of prayer has become so tangible for us!

Merry Christmas and we wish you as deep and joyful a celebration of the season of Christ's birth as our family will have!

Love,
Glenn (& Mary)

II
Poetry 2008

My Brother
(July 15, 2008)

He enters, unannounced, unseen
        like a vapour
My only visitor this first night
        of my new hell

And he is there, quiet, rock-carved,
        pock-marked, disconjugate-gazed
He is here in his unique abundance

If our world is predominantly
        recto-linear, with some circles
        and curves added
then he moves as a triangular
        soul, wedging and slipping
        through, never understood
        nor staying too long, always
        seeming out-of-place

And yet here he is on my first
        night, welcomer of despair,
        quiet comforter, carefully
        wearing the t-shirt I gave
        him at Easter

He looks worried, but does
        not address the concern
He last sat with us the
        morning after my surgery
        at another hospital
        and quietly was, then too

"This is a longer way to come"
"I have a bus pass now … I'm
        on Welfare for the first
        time" (quieter)

He hands me his pass, and
     the picture shows a black
     eye
"Oh, my brother and I had a
     bit of a fight the night before"

But I am your brother, your
     only brother
There is your other unknown, genetically-linked
     loosely-parametered family

Do you fit anywhere, my triangular-
     souled friend and brother?
You are, after all, just another
     fuckin' Injun no matter
     where you are, here or
     in the North

You leave the $9 per hour cook's
     job when the prejudice mounts
     and just slip away
"He was just another fuckin'
     Injun … better he's gone"

So, you sit here with us in this
     broom-closet of a room,
     quietly listening to the mechanical
     grind of the IV,
     just being

And you look worried
     your rock-cliffed face shows
     uneasy eyes that move with concern
You are quick to smile as always
     but dampened with quiet dis-ease

And yet, my brother, you are the
        one who has suffered
You bear scars untold, you
        hear the hatred around the
        corner, you see the fear
        as people regard you

It is I who admire you!
I look up to your strength and
        internal stature!
I am humbled by the warmth
        and truth in your triangular soul!

The mistiness you carry about
        your granite-hewn countenance
        is simply beauty
        in its simplest
        rawest
        form

In many ways, my dear brother,
        you are for me the
        archetype of
        creation
living, breathing, sitting beside me
        in this god-damned little room

Prose: 2008

Hello all,

Mary and I were in London today. Dr. Y., the surgeon I originally saw last year, referred me to an ENT/plastic surgeon to look at reconstructing my nasal passageways (it's all the rage these days!). Radiation has left me with no passageway on the right and very limited on the left. This isn't the end of the world, but it is problematic ... I have to mouth-breath always, which leaves me extra dry on top of limited saliva production ... I also can't properly clear my sinuses, leaving me chronically congested ... which all leads to some difficulty with eating, sleeping, etc.

None of this is unmanageable, just unpleasant and hard on the old mouth and nasal zones.

So, we saw Dr. R. at St. Joe's in London today (always good to be back in a Sisters of St. Joseph hospital!). I had a CT scan first thing and then saw the consultant. He carefully took us through the scan, which looks excellent. It was extremely reassuring to us to actually see the scan, not just read a radiology report. Really things look wonderfully clear, except for my nose, and the strange boney changes on the right side of my face are all consistent with post-radiation remodelling (these are only changes that can be felt, as opposed to seen).

He was so impressed with how blocked my nose is that he invited Mary to have a look when I was being examined. I am planning to sell tickets for those who would like to stare up my nostrils, apparently an exciting event. Dr. R. says he can definitely fix things with endoscopic surgery, and at the same time do multiple biopsies to rule out any cancer (this is the best follow-up test possible - testing the tissue itself - only possible with the nose being opened up again). Despite booking his surgeries for Feb. 2009 (!!) at present, he wants to squeeze me in in the next 2-3 months. I will miss 2 weeks of work, but we are very keen to proceed.

I see the radiation oncologist (Dr. H.) in a couple of weeks. He has been rather unhelpful to us in the post-treatment phase. We still need to explore what is the right kind of testing for me for surveillance - likely PET scanning, which has some political problems in Ontario. My consultation with Dr. R. today will be helpful in approaching Dr. H. as well.

All-in-all an excellent day, despite the overwhelming spring weather!

Love,
Glenn

Date: May 14, 2008
Subject: health update & 2008 relay for life

So, dear friends, here we are writing a note for the 2008 Relay for Life. You may remember our families' extraordinary involvement in last year's inaugural Guelph Lake event: TEAM CURE (a.k.a. us) contributed almost $23,000 of the $85,000 raised - and there were 35 teams involved!

I am still here, doing well, a little streamlined and short of hair, some perma-tan, and more actively teasing my kids than ever. I am still here - body, soul, and mind … more or less intact, a few little problems, but some things actually functioning better than ever. Last summer, I wasn't here. I was so sick and decimated by the treatment that I was barely existing. This is the plight for many cancer patients, but the reality is never appreciated until it hits you (and I pray it never does).

Mary was magnificent; and if anyone was heroic, it was she. Theo and Henry, always marvellously adaptive, were the continual positives through my strange daily ritual of being driven to London and coming back sick as a … well, I wouldn't wish it on a dog.

You listened to the various chapters of my story last year, and, thank God, here we are, living life to the fullest and quite thankful as new chapters continue to unfold. Perhaps this year's relay is even more important to us than in 2007. I will be able to participate through the night (or at least one of my brothers-in-law can carry me if I fall asleep … they would, you know!). And this year's event is truly a celebration. I have a small surgery scheduled 2 weeks before and will be off work a short while. A rather talented ENT/plastic surgeon in London will be reopening my nasal passageways, which will allow me to breathe normally again, preserve my limited salivation, and also get sinus biopsies for the first time since my treatment. I may be a little bruised and battered at the time of the relay, but it won't hold me back.

I continue to work part-time, though slowly increasing, sing with Tactus, run around with the kids (they're faster than me), and smell the roses (with improved olfactory sense coming soon).

Please consider making a donation to the Canadian Cancer Society through the Relay for Life. There is only upside to this. We've both written interesting introductions on our webpages, and included up-to-date photos (Mary more beautiful than I, as you will see - but this has always been the case!). You will receive a tax receipt with the same level of professionalism that the CCS always promotes. If you wish to honour someone in your life, consider buying a luminary. They are lit at dusk and give a magical effect to the track throughout the night (see Mary's sister Laura's illustration below). Make a donation soon, our event is just around the corner!

With much appreciation,
Glenn & Mary

Date: May 31, 2008
Subject: health update post-operative

Dear friends,

Here I am emailing you again, just after I promised not to! Three days ago I was pestering you one last time about the Relay for Life, and now I need to let you know about my surgery on Thursday.

Mary's and my primary anxiety heading into this reconstructive surgery was biopsies that would be taken for the first time since my treatment last year. Because of the scarring, my original surgeon was unable to get biopsies last Fall, as he had wished. All the imaging (3 CT scans and 1 MRI) over the past 7 months have not shown disease, but within the limits of the technology. These tests cannot adequately determine the difference between treatment effects (scarring, inflammation) and possible disease. Unfortunately my surgeon discovered a small tumour on Thursday, and the biopsy showed that it was cancer.

This is the same cancer as originally, and it is residual … I was likely never truly in "remission". I know I am being somewhat technical with my language, but I do need you to properly understand the situation. Your understanding gives great relief to me, as there is absolutely no reason for you to start writing your sympathy cards to Mary (if you get my drift!).

This is the deal: we won the original battle in this war; my enemy was "95%" defeated, which left 5% of the enemy remaining unbeknownst to us; this 5% has regrouped, grown a little, and engaged in some guerilla warfare – and we have just discovered this - time for the second battle.

This is very typical for head & neck cancers. They don't tend to metastasize (spread farther afield) the way other cancers can. They do tend to need multiple treatments. We always knew that surgery was a possibility after the chemo and radiation. And, to tell the truth, I am now stronger both mentally and physically to withstand this next challenge. I apologize for the military language, not usually my cup-of-tea, but cancer treatment is war. War against invading cells that are not you – that are a corruption of your DNA, a false self and invading force.

We feel strong about this next phase of battle, and pray that it is the defining treatment in my progression towards cure. We need to move quickly now, CT/MRI/PET scan hopefully this week … new surgical consult as well. And hopefully treatment as soon as possible.

Don't get me wrong, this is not welcome stress. Mary and I and our families have had a difficult past 48 hours. But, Mary and I and Theo and Henry can cope with the stress – we have before – it is strangely familiar territory for us, and yet not of the magnitude we experience last winter and spring. Plus, we have always quietly wondered if the remission were real, and now we know … remember 'tis "better to know thine enemy".

So, dear friends, I look forward to not belabouring you with news like this. I intend on sharing with you news of our future anniversary celebrations, of Theo and Henry's accomplishments, news of life's bounty. I fully intend to keep teasing my children well into their adult years. I certainly don't believe that life is purposeless, nor do I believe that we are subject to suffering by divine whim or for a specific task in learning. The beauty of creation comes through in magnificent ways – when we visited the Grand Canyon last winter (just before my diagnosis), when we slipped our toes into the salty warmth of the Atlantic Ocean late on a February evening this year (it was pitch dark and we could only hear and feel the sea), when I step into King's College Chapel (where I must take T&H), when our family arrives at our beloved cottage on the Bruce and we absorb Lake Huron's vastness – these are the large-scaled, stone-founded, broadly-etched signs of creation. But it is the small stuff, the delicate and fragile, where creation lives and breathes – when I sing Bach, when I see my child making music for others, when I watch my wife nurse me, when I speak with someone who has a broken heart, when I am more bones than flesh – this allows the magnificence of it all … without the potential for failure, for suffering, for imperfection, it would all be false reality, a world of automatons, a Lego-built existence.

Love always abides, though we do only see through a glass, darkly; someday we will understand these things clearly, not now (but love does see and carries us on).

The quality of mercy is not strain'd,
It droppeth as the gentle rain from heaven
Upon the place beneath: it is twice blest;
It blesseth him that gives and him that takes:
'Tis mightiest in the mightiest: it becomes
The throned monarch better than his crown;
His sceptre shows the force of temporal power,
The attribute to awe and majesty,
Wherein doth sit the dread and fear of kings;
But mercy is above this sceptred sway;
It is enthroned in the hearts of kings,
It is an attribute to God himself;
And earthly power doth then show likest God's
When mercy seasons [all things] …

Shakespeare, from The Merchant of Venice

Date: July 13, 2008
Subject: the next update

Hello again dear friends,

Recently I began an email with the proviso that what was to follow would be less than succinct. I make the same promise here.

I've never been drawn to rollercoaster rides, but we have certainly been on one these past few weeks since I last communicated with you. (And I still don't like them!) Our lives have been truly chaotic over this time. I have chosen very specifically not to send out an email until now. First, we have been too engrossed in the rollercoaster journey. Second, the trip has been too undifferentiated, the path too uncertain, too unclear to give you a coherent, reasonable message.

As of Tuesday, this has changed. As to the rollercoaster, it of course started with the diagnosis of recurrent cancer in my sinus at the end of May. The story of a small tumour recurrence rapidly devolved over the next week. On June 4th I had a series of CT scans from head to abdomen, routine "staging" for cancer, and that same evening travelled into Toronto for an MRI of my head. We were most focused on the MRI, which seemed the critical test to evaluate the state of the sinus tumour. The next day I heard from my friend and sage oncologist from Cambridge that the CT of my chest was abnormal and metastasis (cancer spread) could not be ruled out.

We were gobsmacked, to say the least. I had absolutely no respiratory symptoms and we had never considered the chance of spread. This was the day before the Relay for Life at Guelph Lake and what was billed as a new year for TEAM CURE after my participation last year on the precipice of mounting treatment illness. Nonetheless, we had a fabulous weekend. TEAM CURE raised virtually the same amount as last year – $22,000 – first place to second's $6000. I raised $8000 myself, thanks to all of you!

Mary and I have become experts by necessity at packaging up stress and functioning in life. This has proven an incredibly useful trait, especially now. This is not the same as burying one's head in the sand, but allows us to continue to live despite mounting unpredictability and more potentially bad news. It took some sorting on our part, but between consulting a new head & neck surgeon at Princess Margaret Hospital, reconsulting my previous medical oncologist in London, and connecting with my radiation oncologist, we started to see what the path would be. It is, of course, wonderful to have the support of many friends, but it is indeed a blessing to have some friends with good connections – my colleague in Cambridge and Mary's cousin who is a radiation oncologist in Thunder Bay. Their unadulterated and concerned advice has been so helpful to us.

Two things were clear: I needed a chest biopsy to determine what the abnormal finding was, and I needed special expertise and a comprehensive opinion. The surgeon in Toronto arranged the biopsy, performed with a new less-invasive technique; and we arranged a multidisciplinary assessment at the University of Pittsburgh Medical Centre, a world-leading institution in head & neck cancer. Mary had been in touch with a marvellously responsive oncologist there over the past 6 months as she researched the best surveillance plan for my care. He and two colleagues saw me June 26th – a totally worthwhile time for us. In the span of one day I was assessed in a manner that our Canadian system, as much as it saddens me to say, cannot provide. We were treated with utter grace and consideration, never dehumanized. The team at UPMC engaged in the kind of "out-of-the-box" thinking that my case requires, and we came home with our hopes enlivened and further good sketchings of a plan.

Just before leaving for Pittsburgh we found out that, as we had expected, my chest biopsy was positive for cancer. So, this is not good. But we were prepared. This information formalized the fact that surgery could not be part of the treatment picture at present, and that systemic therapy was the choice. This means chemo, which itself involves a host of options. Thankfully my medical oncologist in London is one of those rare "out-of-the-box" thinkers as well.

Our objective coming back from UPMC was to settle on a treatment plan and hopefully accomplish all or most of it in Ontario. We applied for out-of-country funding for going to Pittsburgh from the Ministry of Health and, shock of shocks, were approved. This sets a standard for possible care in Pittsburgh if a necessary treatment is not available here. But for now, and as of last Tuesday, we have the plan I need.

Tomorrow I start an intensive chemo regimen in London. The problem with standard head & neck therapies is that they are geared towards an aged, smoking and alcohol abusing population with significant medical problems pre-existing, like COPD and heart disease. Well, I am none of the above (quiet in the cheap seats please). The chemo I will be receiving is geared towards a patient with metastatic testicular cancer (even more quiet in the cheap seats now). This is an approach that oncologists use for men my age with life-threatening cancer but otherwise good health. Added into this mix will be one of the new "biological" drugs which are looking like the future of treatment for certain cancers. I will get 4 rounds of this every 3 weeks and will be in hospital for 5 days each time. These are very toxic medications with serious side-effects, so I will be closely monitored and treated for problems as necessary.

To be honest, we are feeling good about this. We've been through our emotional turmoil and there will be more to come. But the specific plan feels so right after all of the stress and work of the past six weeks. We are in "practical mode" presently, which is completely fine for us.

In the past two weeks we have received many messages inquiring about our state of affairs. We cannot return every message and cannot explain this situation over and over – it is too complicated and too exhausting. In fact, life is not just about my cancer in our household. Theo had her 11th birthday Friday and we've spent the weekend at the cottage with two of her friends celebrating and inaugurating the new treehouse (it's one serious structure). Henry performed in his day camp's operetta Friday night, and Theo just finished a week of drama camp. Mary has been coordinating a meticulous and miraculous restoration of our 120 year old front portico. I have been organizing coverage of my practice and have been blessed with a lovely pair of doctors looking for just the kind of work that I'm offering. The truth is it's hard for me to know when and how I will return to work, but I am anticipating at least 6 months off (again). I am reading, and pole-pruning on the island, thinking, and gardening at home, playing a little baseball with the kids, eating as many of Mary's delicious calories as possible. I still cannot drink wine because of my post-radiation mouth, but I have invested some research into the Ontario craft brewery industry … and plan more research as I am able!

My major illness last year was due to radiation, and this is not part of the current plan. I am anticipating fatigue and risk of infection as my major problems upcoming. This is familiar territory, which is helpful. And I am alive, and actively teasing Theo and Henry (and Mary for that matter). Our life is spiritually engaged like never before and this is rich territory, very rich. My wealth is my friends, life's relationships, and the unparalleled support of a family without peer, both Peirsons and Beingessners. I love them all dearly and receive as much or more in reciprocation.

My brain feels sharper than ever. My heart feels larger. My soul more connected to what is essence in life. These, my friends, are gifts. My advice: seek these gifts now and do not cease, do not wait for the clarity of tragic circumstances.

Henry's obsession (difficult to keep track) this winter has been all matters shipwreck, especially the great steamliners, and especially the Titanic after Theo's superb speech in grade 5. Perhaps you've heard of it? The Titanic?? Big ship, invincible, tragic accident … sorry. The great steel ship heading full bore for the iceberg is a perfect metaphor for our life at present. We see the disaster coming and now, thankfully, know that the engines will be put into full reverse. This is the first objective. Then we will worry about the next direction on our voyage. But first, stop the inevitable path towards that iceberg.

Cancer is a disease of cells, not tumours. It is insidious, ubiquitous. It is the bastardization of a normal cell into false reality, an aggressive, fast-reproducing, invasive unit of not-you. The Canadian Cancer Society trumpets its motto as striving for a cancer-free world. As much as I respect the organization, this aim is fundamentally misguided. Cancer is a reality of our human structure, of our genetic blueprint, our creation. It is a necessary frailty of this wondrous structure called the human body. The aim should be preventing cancer as much as possible, treating for cure when possible, and attempting solutions that allow life with cancer, as a chronic disease, as something manageable, containable. This is now our hope for me. My disease does not look curable, but we do hold out hope of a miracle. We are content with extending life, and a quality of life at that.

I have stated in this past year that as long as I survive the disease, I will be thankful for the ultimate-perspective giving experience of cancer. Well, it is my reality. It has become my unwanted companion, a persistent invader, full of threat and the worst consequences. Am I angry? No. Am I mad at anything or anybody? No. Am I trapped in despair? No. Without hope? Never. Have I lost anything? Yes, but I have gained more in return. Am I anxious for Mary, for Theodora, for Henry? Yes, deeply, as deeply as possible. Am I anxious for myself? Yes, for the possible loss of my reality, watching my children grow into the fullness of their potential. But I am not anxious about death. It is no foe. It will come for us all and I do not fear its transition. But I am willing to wait, and hopeful to not see it in my room for some time to come.

What has become almost cliché in Paul's writing from Corinthians lives as truth for me: "So now faith, hope, and love abide, these three; but the greatest of these is love." But I do beg to differ in small degree. There is none greater – love, faith, and hope live intertwined for us, equally real and important, not divorceable one from another.

As moved, I will keep you posted, and promise to be more succinct next time!

Glenn

The Message

A message from God
delivered by a bird
at my window, offering friendship.
Listen. Such language!
Who said God was without
speech? Every word an injection
to make me smile. Meet me,
it says, tomorrow, here
at the same time and you will remember
how wonderful today
was: no pain, no worry;
irrelevant the mystery if
unsolved. I gave you the X-ray
eye for you to use, not
to prospect, but to discover
the unmalignancy of love's

growth. You were a patient, too,
anaesthetised on truth's table,
with life operating on you
with a green scalpel. Meet me, tomorrow,
I say, and I will sing it all over
again for you, when you have come to.

R.S. Thomas

Dear family,

It is probably a very good juncture to give all of you an update on my health. Mary and I were in London again on Monday. This time just for a review with my oncologist, our beloved Dr. W., and no chemo (no more chemo, thanks very much). He is pleased with the state of my health and happy not to be taking me to the edge of extreme unpleasantness with his treatments any longer. My hemoglobin is not great, but we are going to watch this, as it will gradually improve with no further chemo assaults. If it dips lower next week, I will get a transfusion; but this is no big deal, and sometimes it is nice to get the tank filled.

The next big thing on the horizon is a PET-CT scan, a very specific test for my cancer, but unfortunately difficult to access in Ontario. Dr. W. fully supports the necessity of this test and has ordered one in Hamilton (the London machine is down presently). We will see him again in 3 weeks ... if denied in Hamilton, it appears we will need to look at Montreal or Buffalo, and he will help us with organizing this. The pursuit of this test is potentially a major frustration, but we are staying optimistic and will see how it unfolds. PET-CT is crucial in determining whether I need further treatment, likely stereotactic radiation (focal and limited radiation), which would probably happen in Toronto (or possibly Pittsburgh).

But, most importantly, I am in a phase of real recuperation now. Time to eat! For the first time in 4 months, just as I am starting to feel decent, I do not have to reenter chemotherapy. (Hallelujah!!) I had my G-tube removed at the Guelph Hospital today, a rather mechanical experience ... Mary says it looks like I have a bullet hole in my abdomen ... at least there's no exit wound. I should be able to start exercising and put some muscle on soon (not just count on the muscle between my ears).

That's about it, except that we are looking forward to having some fun while enjoying life's little experiences. As most of you know, we took Theo up to the cottage for three days last week while Henry was gallivanting around Venice with my folks. November is busy with the start of Tactus, a concert for Theo in Toronto, and both kids in GYS Christmas concert at the end of the month. I will continue off work for some time yet, but have good arrangements in place.

Love,
Glenn

Dear family,

Mary and I were in London again on Monday (lovely snow squalls on the 401) for a review with Dr. W. and my P-mab infusion. Nothing earth-shattering to report, except that Mary had a lovely gift idea planned out for Dimas until she realized that she doesn't have him on the list this year.

First, hopefully this is the last time for the P-mab treatment in London as arrangements are being made for it to be given in Cambridge (which is every 3 weeks). Second, it looks almost certain that the PET scan test, which I need for proper assessment of disease, will not happen in Ontario. We have applied for out-of-country coverage through OHIP (which we received for the consults in Pittsburgh) and have a date for the test in Buffalo on Dec. 1, which is good timing. Third, Dr. W. completed a number of forms that Mary researched and we are hoping for some drug coverage either through the Trillium plan or from the pharmaceutical company or perhaps both. We have no idea of the chances for this. Unfortunately we are breaking new ground with the P-mab, so creative arguments have to be made as the standard channels don't work.

That's about it. We are busy and having fun and I've put on 5 pounds in the past month (all the way up to 174!). I am enjoying singing again with Tactus and Mary had a book-club retreat just this past weekend. The kids are cresting as per usual and we are keenly anticipating the season of Advent.

I will send out a mass email next week to give a general update, as I've not done that for some time and this should help with the mounting number of well-intentioned queries and questions. Hey, I got together with 2 old (certainly getting old now) friends the other night and watched football, which means mainly chatted, and ate pizza, which means mainly ate pizza. Mary and I are off to the cottage tomorrow to close-up and the kids sing "O Canada" at the Storm game on Friday night ... that is our short-term excitement!

Love,
Glenn

Hello family,

As you know, we were in Buffalo Monday for my PET-CT scan. Aside from a weather-laced drive on Sunday night and being randomly chosen for US border patrol search (unpleasant), everything went smoothly, including the drive home where I was told that I would light up the radiation sensors but we were allowed straight through. Alright, we did have a letter explaining the procedure.

A PET scan involves injection with a radio-isotope, "tagged" glucose, that hyperactive cells will absorb. Cancer cells are the most hyperactive, so as long as one remains very still, has followed the instructions beforehand, and doesn't have other areas of non-cancerous inflammation, the hot spots have a strong chance of indicating cancer activity. The imaging is enhanced by the anatomical CT scan pictures, which are then fused with the PET scanning.

It was a time of some anxiety for us, as this test gives critical information and determines success of treatment thus far and the need for further treatment. To be honest, my feeling heading into the test was that the results would be neutral at best and negative at worst. We had no expectation that I would be in remission at this point. As the radiation oncologist in Pittsburgh suggested, "Blast the tumours into manageable size with chemo, then treat with focal radiation".

The final report, with comparisons to all my other imaging, will take a few days to generate. We did meet with the radiologist after my scan on Monday morning. As expected, there are some very small hotspots ... two in the sinus (much smaller than before I restarted chemo) and three very small spots in the mediastinum, the space between the lungs. So, the good news is that there is nothing new, and what was known appears to be much smaller and likely amenable to some specific radiation techniques. Despite the stress of testing, and multiple medical appointments recently with a nephrologist and new oncologist in Cambridge, we are accepting of this information and ready to look at the next stage.

We wanted to send an update to you, our family, but will not share this information outside this circle until we have spoken with my specialists in London in the next few days. I am still in treatment with the new agent you have previously heard about, P-mab, and starting Monday will be receiving this in Cambridge, which will save driving to less-than-beloved London every 3 weeks. My assessment with the kidney specialist was good, and likely won't require further follow-up.

Presently we don't know where we go from here. There is a decent chance of needing focal radiation further afield, which would mean Pittsburgh. The experience in Canada using limited radiation for head & neck cancer is scanty at best. All this will come to more light in the next little (Mary would emphasize this!) while. You may remember that our first objective was to stop the cancer, and it appears this has happened. And the P-mab continues as ongoing treatment. The next step will be to put the cancer further at bay.

Right now I am rather tired of telling the story to various specialists and would rather focus on Advent, the kids, and my re-found ability to drink beer (great calories). Mary will be happier to have structure around this; and I will let her be tenacious in this regard!

Love,
Glenn

Hello family,

Details of my treatment plan will likely evolve relatively quickly over the next little while. So it is probably better to send you a small rash of emails than wait to announce some grand plan. Speaking of rashes, I have one ... quite a doozy actually. P-mab is notorious for its skin problems, but I've developed hives and a touch of asthma. 15% of P-mab patients get respiratory side-effects ... essentially hives in one's respiratory tract. This responds well to puffer treatment and I am now on some steroids and antibiotics for the acne-effects. All good fun. I joked with the oncologist yesterday that soon my kids would hang ornaments on me and then we wouldn't need a tree!

I will probably need a dose reduction. Interestingly this problem has arisen since the P-mab changed to every 3 weeks after I finished chemo.

Yesterday was the typical long and tiring day in London. From the snow squalls to traffic downtown to the hospital parking lot's automated exit not functioning to ... the dentist at the dental oncology clinic worrying about a possible cancerous lesion in the back of my throat. This just before lunch a 1/2 hour before seeing my radiation oncologist. I felt certain that it was my residual mucositis, but Mary had a look with the dentist and was worried as well. To make a somewhat painful story short, by the time I saw the oncologist there was nothing there ... that's beauty of mucous - just needs a little hacking and spewing for treatment (and I am an expert at this). So it was nothing, a anxious chimera of cancerous intent ... just not an experience we needed. Nonetheless, we were a little giddy when my oncologist had a look in and said, "What is she talking about? I don't see anything!".

We hadn't seen Dr. H. since last June and, though never our favourite, he was relatively good-natured and positively-spirited yesterday. He feels that Toronto may have much to offer in the way of focal radiation for me. He will confer with our beloved Dr. W. on Monday and get back to us mid-week. We also FedEx'd a package to Pittsburgh with all of my recent scans and information. They have a team meeting on Tuesday and will get back to us as well. OHIP is asking for more information from London before deciding on coverage of my Buffalo PET scan. My office has been a bit of a stress recently, but we're off for the annual Christmas luncheon on Friday and that should fix everything (ha!!). Perhaps time for some raises for my staff (along with nice bottles of wine)!

That is that for now. We feel fairly clear-headed and inspirited about the coming Christmas season and even managed to cut our own tree today (as the children balked at decorating me).

We will, of course, see all of you soon and greatly look forward to sharing the season together.

Love,
Glenn

What about Joseph?
(Christmas, 2008)

What about Joseph? The Gospel of Matthew tells us that us that the prophecy was right, Jesus was born out of the family of King David, out of the family of Father Abraham. This was Joseph's family line. Matthew also tells us that Joseph was visited in a dream by an angel: "Do not be afraid to take Mary as your wife, because her baby will be Jesus Emmanuel, which is 'God with us'". And Joseph followed his dream, even though the Holy Spirit was the father of Jesus.

The Story from Luke tells us that King Augustus ruled that the entire Roman world at that time would undergo a census, a counting of the people. So all men were to take themselves and their family to the place of their birth to be registered. Joseph took Mary, his wife-to-be, and travelled from Nazareth to the little town of Bethlehem. Here Mary gave birth to Jesus, and had to wrap him in cloths and use a manger, an animal feeding trough, as a cradle, for they could find no other place to stay.

On the journey towards Christmas, this is all that we know about Joseph. But there is so much more to the story!

Joseph must have been a strong man of heart and mind. In his day, the fact that Mary was pregnant and they were not yet married would have been a terrible thing. Joseph must have found this confusing, but the angel helped him to understand and choose God's path. Of course, telling other people that everything was okay because God was father to Mary's baby would not have helped. Who would believe this? Joseph must have been very quiet and strong in his feelings, his convictions, his trust of Mary and God.

And so they made the journey to Bethlehem, which is a little more than 100 km south from Nazareth. Rocky and dusty, likely cold at night on the roads, hot under the sun during the day, a little money for food but eating just enough, Joseph and Mary walked this distance, perhaps with a donkey to help Mary ride. Joseph would have been in charge, but no map, no street signs, no internet or G.P.S. assistance. Just the flow of people making their way for census, trudging along, struggling with the difficult command of King Augustus. The journey likely took a week or more of long stretches of walking. It would have been slow travel with a pregnant wife. The travel could have been painful for Mary, certainly uncomfortable. They would have both been worried about this strange and wonderful pregnancy. Would this pilgrimage to Bethlehem harm the pregnancy? What would happen when they arrived in the little town? Remember, they couldn't call ahead or book a hotel on-line or arrange a rental car or even book a room at a hospital.

And so finally, with dirty, bruised feet, tired and hungry, with Mary starting to feel more movement in her baby, they arrived in the little town of Bethlehem. Joseph was relieved. All of his fear dropped, "Let's just get a room and rest and we can prepare for the birth if it is to happen soon."

But what happened? There was no place to stay. Nowhere, not one room, no one even offered to share a room. It was dark and Mary was having labour pain. "Please, you must let us have a room! My wife is about to have a baby!" No answer, no care, no concern. Joseph was frightened, more than in any way he had ever been scared, especially since he had met Mary. This strange story from the angel was now going badly. How could Mary give birth to Jesus in the street, on the side of the road?

Joseph was desperate, his eyes were filled with fear and his heart was jumping. He did not want to show Mary his fear, but what to do? Behind the main laneway, behind the mud-walled hotels with locked doors, there was a stable in the side of a hill. It looked clean and warmer, with a roof, straw and some animals. He brought Mary over to the stable: "Mary, let me fix this up. There is clean straw over here. I can cover the mud and animal droppings. It will be warm enough and there is even a manger the babe could sleep in."

"Oh, Mary, I am so sorry, this is not right for any baby, let alone Jesus."

And Joseph quickly cleaned up an area in the stable. The animals stood back, did not complain, and were peaceful with the mysterious scene unfolding in front of them.
And there, in the middle of a small barn, Mary had no choice but to deliver her baby. Joseph worked hard to help, found some water and cloths to help clean Jesus and Mary. Birth is a beautiful and messy process. "Keep Jesus warm," Joseph

thought to himself, "and get him feeding with Mary". Looking around with some desperation still in his eyes, Joseph was feeling like father, husband, protector, soldier to guard his new family.

He did not see the light. It was blazing down from the most extraordinary star just overhead. He could not hear the angels singing to the shepherds in the nearby fields. He could not tell that the animals sensed something special, perhaps the movement of an angel in their midst. He was still too scared knowing that this was not the place for a baby or his exhausted wife.

"Mary, you are safe right now and Jesus seems content. I must run into town and find us a place. Mary, I will be right back. Everything will be fine!"
Joseph ran hard and fast, nearly twisting his ankle, but he was determined to get a proper room. He knocked on the door with the side of his fist: "My wife has just had a baby. We are outside in the stable. We must have a room. We need the clean and safety for our baby!"

No answer. No answer. Joseph hit as many doors as he could find, always the same story, and always no answer or "Go away!". Joseph felt like his heart might jump out of his chest. He was scared and angry and confused and desperate to help Jesus and Mary. He had never felt this way his entire life. But, he had to go back, he had already been away too long. Were they still okay back at the stable?

He turned and pulled his hood over his head, as the wind had come up and the night was cold. He ran, even harder than before. Joseph was crying, not sad but frustrated. This was all wrong … this was all wrong. "And I cannot do anything to help my family!" He could not see anymore, his eyes blurred with tears and his head filled with gloom. He tripped around the corner back to the stable and hit his face onto the mud path.

As he got up, it happened.

There were men with sheep, dirty, dusty men with tattered clothes and long sticks slowly approaching the stable and kneeling. There were many of them. "What are you doing!! Get away from my wife and baby!!" Joseph could take no more, the long journey, no room in the inn, a birth in the stable, and no hospitality in the town. Now all these strangers invading the little, humble space, the only space of safety he had found.

Yes, and then it happened.

An older shepherd at the back placed his hand on Joseph's shoulder: "We have seen the angels, Father, and all is well. We are here to see the Saviour, wrapped in cloths and lying in a manger." And Joseph looked with clear eyes into the beauty of this old withered man's face. "Thank you friend," said Joseph. And he looked up and saw the most amazing thing. Mary was feeding Jesus and they were at peace. The stable was filled with starlight, the animals were kneeling, the shepherds too, and the sky, the rafters, the air, the wind were filled with angels.

"Glory to God and on Earth Peace" the song sang from overhead. Joseph's heart was calmed and his head cleared, just like when the angel had visited him months before. The old shepherd touched his shoulder again. "We are here because Love has been born today for us," he said. "We are here for Love."

III

Poetry 2009

January 20, 2009

Many of our moments are marked
whether anniversary or life-event
whether public or private
we are compelled to mark them
     even if time or date is random or fleeting or trite

So I watched, today, feeling that I ought to
but having little expectation
for anything profound or moving or real
     and I was wrong (again)

For I and we and they were all marking this moment
and it was momentous
     honestly

And I realized that despite the words and ceremony
and pomposity and media magnitude
that it was real and significant
and that the tears on her face
     were genuine

On her black, pock-marked, rough-skinned
     face
rolling down her roughened, toughened, tender
     cheeks
that she was weeping for the moment
     utterly and openly and privately and publicly

And I could as well
down my funny face
my inward existence
     for freedoms lost and freedoms gained

And I realized that for her people
     for many people

it is not a moment of emancipation in any true sense
just as it wasn't when proclaimed some almost
one-hundred fifty years ago
        but the moment is emancipation in spirit

Which is where the tears originate
and the bolts are not necessarily open
nor the doors swung wide
nor the invitation full-hearted
        yet

But the lock is lubricated with hope
and loosened and the key inserted
and the door can be opened
and besides which
        the spirit moves between the bars

We mark the moment of freedom
        new freedom
it is genuine and real and palpable
and the tears are relief, hope attained, dreams gained
and old sadness reclaimed
        and let go
        to be with the freedom
        spirit that interweaves the bars
        moment marked

Breakfasts

(February 7, 2009)

"I've put the water on, why don't you make the coffee now …"
called into the bathroom
"where's my coffee… that's funny I don't smell any coffee… I need some coffee"
persistent niggling, purely for my own entertainment
"Okay, okay, let me just finish up here… tell Henry to eat up, he's being slow…
what is Theo crabbing about now?"
from the bathroom

"I wonder where she gets the morning crabbiness from?"
muttered quietly beside the kettle
("I could, theoretically, grind the beans myself and prep the pot")

"Henry put away your book for now… both of you brush your teeth… he is
coming Theo… Henry tie your laces tight, man!… do not, I repeat, do not say
'THE-O' that way, you know it drives Mummy and Daddy crazy!… Theo he is
coming… bye, have a great day, see you later [kiss, kiss]… don't forget to fart!"

"Don't be so agitated…"
"Arghhh"

"Come make the bed"
from the stairway
"Alright, just relax"

Bed made, coffee brewed, music playing
jams, jellies, Marmite, chestnut paste on the table
"Do you want an egg today?"
"I was just going to ask you"
"How about scrambled… I'll do it… I do a better job"

"Crumpet, toast, both?"

"Both buttered?"
"No peanut butter today"

Sipping from earthenware cups
perfectly runny egg onto plate
crisp buttered toast
more fresh coffee

Music in the background, some Beethoven sonatas
or perhaps some morning Vivaldi
but otherwise silence
beside each other
usual sections of the paper to her left and my right

Occasional shared tid-bit
but otherwise mutual silence
the week-daily ritual
extending beyond its old parameters
by my extended down time

But a marvellous thing
the ritual
the egg
the toast
for me, the Marmite
"Why do you always forget the Lyle's?"
"All I need's the Marmite from that cupboard!"
"Arghh..."

Beautiful little ritual
it's not just the coffee
not just the breakfast
it's all these little elements
woven into a half-hour or so of daily fabric

though the scrambled eggs do have to be just so...

and properly salted
I prefer when just off the pan...

It could be anywhere
(February 7, 2009)

Of course I know that it couldn't be anywhere
but at times I wonder
and this is unsettling
as I am usually a rather settled person

Or at least I used to be
for now when I have a moment with myself
I am not so settled
and that unwelcome emotional nausea can creep in

Sticky stuff, that, creeps and sticks and fills in cracks
fills in bits of space in my life that normally aren't perceived
rest quietly in the background
airy and empty cushions that simply exist and give space

But that nauseated glue can fill the space
thicken life
cloud thoughts and perceptions
and then I wonder if it's here or there, anywhere

A click, cough, drippy eye, spot of numbness,
odd little spot, some blood, achey shoulders,
mucous, mucous,
perhaps the gland is swollen

Is this who I am or have become?
No ..., boldly, never
But, if truth be told, these fearful moments of possession
do happen

And I am not completely in control
but do fight back with more resolve
and push away the sticky nausea
limiting the anywhere

To just a little place
put it away, for now
and do something else
that's not about me

Reading
(February 7, 2009)

Reading has not been easy
these past two years
much reading is operational, functional to daily life
emails, research, communication, notes to self
not an emphasis on pleasure and recreation

A book on poetry criticism was perfect
slow to unfold, every chapter its own entity, no obligation, but intellectually stimulating
A Confederacy of Dunces brilliant but unfinished
still on the back burner
The Christmas Mystery a disciplined and rewarding journey with Henry
just as all the Narnia books have been special

But reading for me, difficult
then this little book, not brilliant, at times amateurish
certainly nothing I would have chosen
a Christmas gift of war-torn prose with a rather
dead-ended (shameless pun) musical illusion

Why would I choose to read about Sarajevo
ordinary people tortured by their awful, shattered existence
their world filled with loss
all have dead loved ones
and more death around the corner

Why am I reading this quickly, perhaps not passionately, earnestly
shouldn't it be a comedy
unchallenging drama
fiction of another reality, distracting?
I don't know, except that the suffering, every character's in the book, is
greater than mine
worse than me

and, I think, I don't feel quite so bad
(not that I dwell on my sadness only, but isn't this the
role of the muse?)

The flower

(February 9, 2009)

the flower opens
translucent petals unfold
when will it wither?

Lois

(March 27, 2009)

on the gift to Theodora of her Great-Grandmother's concert violin

What a hoot, the old coot
she is after all these years
resonating from box of old rosin-clotted cloth
neglected in suspended animation

Great grandmother, she, very fine indeed
strange as unmaternal mother
yet perhaps now mothering
speaking her gift
after restoration

Amber-hued, polished wood
looking young and old
at the same time
as I'm sure she always did

Brittle veneer, supple and strong
beautiful even before sounding
serious instrument
she was and is now

Again, silly old coot
gifted and resonating
in different hands but
same verdict
"Oh …

Lovely instrument, very lovely"
Yes, I'll have a look for
just a minute
becomes
five, ten, fifteen
"Oh …

Wish that I had a little more time"
with her

She speaks, resonates
immediately clearly
no dusty voice
fresh, incisive, prominent treble
rich but subdued lower register
filling the room with
a scale
then Bach
some Paginini, Brahms, Handel
and then Bach

"Perhaps the strings a little close together
at the bridge …
perhaps a little more rounding
to give more separation"

No more separation, though,
the old coot,
she's back
though never was gone
just silent

Too many years quiet
and now she speaks
the old coot
crazy
mother
gifted

And this is beauty
just that
beauty
polished resin-wooded music
of little girl in nymph dress
in 1924 and 2009,
the old coot

THE POOL PLAYERS.
SEVEN AT THE GOLDEN SHOVEL.

We real cool. We
Left school. We

Lurk late. We
Strike straight. We

Sing sin. We
Thin gin. We

Jazz June. We
Die soon.

Gwendolyn Brooks (1960)

MR. A's PLAYERS.
TWENTY-EIGHT AT THE CENTRAL SCHOOL.

We real cool. We
Go school. We

Grade Six. We
No hicks. We

Learn big. We
Brain dig. He

Teach cool. We
No fool.

Glenn Peirson, for Mr. Anderson's class, Central School (2009)

Defining

(April 1, 2009)

Cancer may redefine your life
>   or cause you to do so

>   but it does not define you

It is not you, by definition
>   in fact it is the anti-you

It may invade, destroy, usurp
>   your physical self
may distort, cloud, hijack
>   your mind
may jaundice and weaken
>   your emotional state

>   but it does not touch your spirit
>   cannot affect your soul

Easter People
(April 12, 2009)

We are all an Easter people,
even if not religious in any particular way
or perhaps not at all.

The Christians tend to celebrate Easter-peopled-ness,
not in any proud or holier-than-thou manner,
but as an optimistic promise
resurrection-claiming
Holy Week unwinding
Lent minimizing
kind of way.

But, we are all an Easter people,
at least we Canadians
save those in Victoria or Point Pelee.

Everywhere else, in this often frigid place,
and some of those Scandinavian places too,
Siberia maybe, and Greenland (ha!),
we and they are Easter people.

We live the life of rebirth,
relife, rekindled in our frozen ground,
crocus, snowdrop, scilla,
poking through winter's death
every early Spring.

Coincident with Easter,
resurrected even if forgotten bulb,
springs to life
just like our dead God.

And the Easter person?
Gets that little itch,

behind your garden boot,
near your secateur trigger,
off the rake's handle,
by the soil-spiculed-spade tip,
to go out into your garden of rebirth,
even when the late winter wind says no.

We are an Easter people,
not by choice or faith or creed
but by necessity of digging
tenderly beside that budding bulb
enjoying sun's lengthening,
bicycling children,
snow's disappearance.

Death is swallowed up in Spring garden,
rocks rolled away
revealing many gods alive
reborn
resurrected
and poking their holy, haloed greening heads
through the crumbly soil.

We are an Easter people,
hallelujah,
the angel reassures us that life is …
out in the garden,
we are not alone
winter is over
and the crocus
has come again.

Mr. Bentley
(April 18, 2009)

Perhaps he didn't hear his own name when the Lord called
perhaps the quiet little boy was called
but perhaps it was by another name
just between Samuel and God
      perhaps it was …
      perhaps …

        "Mr. Bentley"

I think of God as a more formal creature anyway,
not so much next-door-neighbour, dear friend
more as Creator, beyond all knowing
      so likely being addressed by God
      could be more formal

        "Mr. Bentley"
        "Mr. Bentley, Samuel," I respond

We furtively smile each time
throughout the evening
with each repeated conversational shard

Perhaps I, the Eli, consider Mr. Bentley as code,
representative of a conversational angle, if he could,
a glimmer of his world, reaching out with this fragment
for something larger
from which he is prevented

And yet, when I listen, it is simply

        "Mr. Bentley"

An offering without strings
gladly met and received with stereotyped response

"Mr. Bentley, Samuel"

And we wonder of this little old boy man
where he is, exactly,
how he fits in our orderly
highly communicated
over-informed world

Science tells us that he is blocked,
trapped in his own neurological reality
without the tools, the synaptic paths
that allow, encourage relational life

Yet the Lord calls Samuel
and he listens, responds,

"Mr. Bentley"

At one point he quietly, as in all things,
reaches over and carefully inspects the cuff
of my suit jacket with his fingers

He listens, in his way, to all the Mozart, Dancla, Bach,
Beethoven and Kabelevsky,
which sounds like two inharmonious cats,
through the evening

The church is warm in April and the pews Calvinist
I slip off my jacket in a moment of self-preservation
And my furtive friend, keeper of Mr. Bentley,
soon thereafter touches the lifeless cuff again
where it sits folded on my lap

He's comparing the jacket on and off me
        I briefly think
touching inert objects, human or not,
        and then it all changes

"Mr. Bentley"
"Mr. Bentley"

His fingers stroke my wrist, where the cuff lay before,
and slowly up my arm to the short-sleeved cuff
gentle, methodical
and I would say lovingly

Perhaps others would categorize this as automatic,
patterned behaviour
but I looked down to my friend
his opalescent eyes, clear, unmoved
and he continued upwards
caressing his hand graciously
        openly, with soft palm
        against my cheek

        "Mr. Bentley"

He had blessed me
in that moment
perhaps sensing my struggle through the evening
pews providing no relief

And I am glad to have sat beside this man of
different dimension
who lovingly anointed me
        in the name and spirit of

        "Mr. Bentley"
        Indeed, Samuel, "Mr. Bentley"

O vos omnes
(Good Friday, April 10, 2009)

Can I, dare I compare my suffering to His?
    Egocentric almost, misplaced
    A touch of grandeur, to my little world of affliction
Compared with all sin, upon His shoulders and bones,
    Hung high with ridicule and derision
    Stripped bare on that naked wood,
    Nailed unjustly to that forsaken hill of skull,
    Empty sockets of rock, waiting for demise of Him
        who is source of love and creation

How do I dare compare with His?

I do not, and yet like Paul I now participate more fully
    In this passion
As in Galatians, "I have been crucified with Christ …"
    And yet my suffering worsens with consciousness
    That I am crucifier, not just crucified

And yet I am not possessed, obsessed by sin,
    But know its presence in my living
    And dying

Yet I stand against the Blameless One, and
    Wonder if my suffering is His suffering
    Ponder if my sorrow be His sorrow

And consolation comes to me, like anointing

For His suffering is not like mine,
    Mine is His

He suffers then and now because of my distress
    He takes my brokenness and drinks of my affliction
    I am drawn in to Him and perfect care given me

For once again, my lesson is not suffering, humility, nor giving over
    But rather, again, it is
    Love

Dispensed in bread and cup, in bone and blood, in gift of the
    Spirit, Holy Ghost, my comforter, consoler,
    Lover of my very soul

And as the great hymn sings today, "Lord, let me never, never
    Outlive my love to thee".

Galatians 2:20 (New International Version)
20 I have been crucified with Christ and I no longer live, but Christ lives in me.
The life I live in the body, I live by faith in the Son of God, who loved me and
gave himself for me.

Antiphon:
O vos omnes qui transitis per viam:
attendite et videte si est dolor sicut dolor meus.

Responsory:
O vos omnes qui transitis per viam, attendite et videte:
    Si est dolor similis sicut dolor meus.
V. Attendite, universi populi, et videte dolorem meum.
    Si est dolor similis sicut dolor meus.

Antiphon:
O all ye that pass by the way,
attend and see if there be any sorrow like to my sorrow.

Responsory:
O all ye that pass by the way, attend and see:
    If there be any sorrow like to my sorrow.
V. Attend, all ye people, and see my sorrow:
    If there be any sorrow like to my sorrow.

...in a note to his mother after she had read the first writing and commented on the final line: Lord, let me never, never / Outlive my love to thee, Glenn wrote:

> *This line struck me, too, as I was singing it and I realized how impossible this would be... to outlive my love for Him. There's eternity in those words. This is beyond words and anathema to those without faith.*

The Cove
(April 28, 2009)

Tourist's trap
round the bend to picture postcard
stacked lobster traps
primary colour shingled shacks on stilts
black indigo water salty cold
rippling sun from freshest breeze

Ready for miniature plastic reproductions
Peggy's Cove made in China
lighthouse keychain or tea towel
Cap Cod gray ice cream shop
parking lot where once stood
little wood houses
where fishermen lived with real families
and smell-sodden clothes
stiff with sweat, salt and codguts

The modern sensibility
acute and skeptical
prepared to reject
manufactured touristic traps
steps out onto granite-hewn landscape
peppered with quartz
massively rounded
obstacle to ocean's break
splashed with pink limestone
sprayed with salty spindrift

Breathtaking, utterly breathtaking
salty air into jaundiced lungs
nature wins over any chance of nonchalance
She is spectacular
sun-splashed massive granite
ocean breakers rolling out to unending sea

undulating beauty under foot
beyond mind's eye

Brain cannot trap the spectacle
and so to walk around, along her
gives slight sense of majesty worthy of
all the guidebook accolades

You should go to Peggy's Cove
despite that everyone has been or says you should
you should

Fairy Troll
(February 15, 2009)

She my funny-faced fairy
         self-proclaimed troll
but then she plays
fairy-music alights
nary a trace of trollness

Dancing and twirling
naked except for her violin
gracefully graciously leading the procession
of mesmerized souls

She is clad in outer garments of
         melody and harmony
but inner, she is music herself
St. Cecilia puffing on cigarette at break
         and breaking our hearts with poignancy
         music's sympathy
filling the chamber of the hall
filling the chamber of our minds
         with sheer beauty, breathed so easily
         it seems
         from our fairy troll

From the pinnacle of music's mountain
she shows no distress
just fluency and poise as she caroms down its path
         a chaconne of movement and play and pathos
then to the lightness of musical humour
         rhythmic play, she demures
"I am no fairy to dance, alone, to the front"
         she laughs, teases herself
"More the troll, I am"

Such an exquisite troll, I do not know
to play with the gift of music's muse
to move in perfect harmony with Cecile
to shift time with melody's part
        leaving dreamily lost the listener's heart

Good troll, do tell if you are not to dance
then what is it you do when music moves
        through you, through us
you weep and weave and waft a sound
of such beauty, purity and purpose bound

You are no troll, though self-proclaimed
more godly than goblin, I maintain
in fact I shout from mountaintop
        She is my fairy queen
        with red-haired mop
the very incarnation of Venetian priest
music's verve and harmony's beast
dream of Purcell's ritornello
more than this I shall call and bellow

She embodies his gift when bow to string
she lifts her violin and makes it sing
Bach's tune, his line, his divine aria
creating simple from complex via
        her gift, her muse, her spark, Cecilia

Music alights from whence it came
from the gods, to gods again
the Bard gifts us with poetry's line
        our fairy queen converts it to divine

How to Say
(May 24, 2009)

The way to say "I love you" to someone
        is to say "I love you" to that person
This has come to my attention
        recently
"I love you" means "I love you"
        and merits
        being said
        to the person
        for whom you feel that love

Various gestures and clipped phrases
        do not
        actually
        say "I love you"

As lovely as a home-cooked casserole
        or cheque for some needed money
        or gift certificate for an indulgence
        is
and is loving, nurturing, caring

It is not the same as saying
        "I love you"
it is not

"Love ya'" or "You're my girl"
        or "You're the best wife, mother, daughter"
        or some Hallmark equivalent
        is
nice and perhaps true

But it is not the same as saying
        "I love you"

Do not mistake a gesture for the
        declaration of love
nor heavy sentiment for its
        clear articulation

Do not misjudge the brevity
        of our existence
in missing the opportunity to say
        "I love you"

Nor misjudge the simplicity of the
        clear statement
with empty blathering, over-repetition
        to meaninglessness

Do not wait until your voice has dried
        and your sunken eyes
        mournfully cry "I love you"

Do not wait until your deathbed
        or someone else's

Do not give expression to love
        in the heat of passion
        nor as an act of contrition

Like any real gift, give expression
        freely, under no duress,
        with no sense of obligation
        or awkward burden

Tell all those that you love
        that you love them
not just your spouse, your lover,
        your beloved

Tell them now or certainly soon

Say to each person that you truly love,
  where your mutual love
  is a bond beyond
  the nature of an ordinary relationship,

"I love you"

For the only way to do this
  I know
The only way to say "I love you" to someone
  is to say "I love you"

Snowy Song Sonnet

(May 26, 2009)

Snow slides silently along slate-edged eaves
slip-streams up through old soffit ice-stiff breeze
into inner sanctum's warm rafters waft
few flakes circle buoyant in song aloft

Contented nature dances as choir sings
carols below that rise and glow and ring
against stone walls and plaster ceiling bring
early December's cold to tempering

Treble voices soar up to descant's reach
echoing harp, organ swell capture each
note in darkest night's flick'ring candlelight
warmth of heart, gleam of carol making bright
our season's spirit, gift of music giv'n
ceremon'al beauty lifts and is ris'n

S'another Snowy Song sort'of Sonnet
{reinterpreted}
(May 29, 2009)

Snow slides silently slipping slowly slate-sledged sleuthing
looking laughing longing lightly lowering little loophole
frosted flake flickering fickle fiddling flowstream
jumping joining jousting jollily joists gem-like jewel

Warm wafting wind waits willingly waiting watching
snatches sad snowflake sillily slithering sideways
choir's carol catches crown's cold cobble calmly creating
melting moistness moment's momentum magically messily

dripping down draft's direction dropping drippily dropping drops
        ... done

Motherf'er

(a response to cancer)
(June 4, 2009)

You know the motherfucker?
Not the time for self-pity
      I say in response
      to the motherfucker

So easy to conjure pity now
      to collect and wallow
      and immerse in it

But this is designed by the motherfucker
      to suck my energy in distraction
      you mothersucker

I'm not angry
just calling a fucker a fucker
      It helps

Declare the truth and fuck the fucker
      It's not my nature
      usually
      to fuck around so freely

But it is her nature
      the motherfucker
      Go fuck yourself
      and stop fucking with me

I say

Nothing wrong with tears
      when you're being fucked
      Just don't let her know or
      have any pleasure
      in my dis-ease
the fucking disease

Go fuck yourself
        Stop mucking with me

My mucky eye is not sad
        you see
It's winking at you
        saying f-you
        you mother fucker you

In the corner

(June 7, 2009)

Dank peeling far corner of the garage
Neglected, unneeded things stack against
mildewed drywall scratched through by some rodent
once upon a time
Standing upon dimly lit cracked concrete into the corner
leaning like an unwanted stack of memories

Memories unstacking from a contained corner
dustily neglected by purpose
Unable to interrupt recollection anymore
the unwanted stack grows and collects
fingerprints from being held involuntarily

Clawing, scratching sounds
dig through my head
grinding and resonating
from flesh cut and pulled
out from the boney corners

Memory left in place,
same corner of my mind,
mildew cleared from other
images stacked against false walls

Unknown past digging into hidden corners
hemorrhaging memory onto antiseptic floor
splitting concrete underneath
Swept into the corner
where I cannot walk by without remembering

Plastic trays that stack for ease of washing
stink of detergent and frozen carrots
The sight of which
I cannot see without remembering

Vinyl-seated waiting rooms
all nauseating and unavoidable
stack in front of me
with Chatelaine and Maclean's
pushed into a corner
where I cannot forget

Moist edge of interstitial swelling
prick and push over and again
until clear connection flowing freely
into the corner of my arm

Rolled from the corner into the
middle of the room
sitting memory of concrete bits
pushed out painfully
bit by bit I can't forget

Long drives from our corner to theirs
monotonous and predictable
kilometres of memory
nauseated necessity

Dark corner out-of-the-way so close
neglected by choice but clawed through
dug open like a wound unhealing
Now I cannot seem to stay
out of that corner
close up the wall
nor keep it dry
Memories seep unpleasantly
through the back of the garage
pushing over ignored stacks
of unwanted things

Poetic ideas come and float
(June 18, 2009)

Poetic ideas float in and float out
on a stream of consciousness or un-   [un-/unopened]
    opened some stay while others are explored
      etched with pencil or sometimes slathered with thick colour-   [colour/colourful/full]
full ideas which never attain the possibility
of your mind's eye

I do not claim to understand this strange process
offerings from the muse which may bring forth-   [forth right/forthright]
    right (or wrong) musings in the poet
      where beauty may emerge or a certain flat-   [flat-/flatfootedness/footedness]
footedness, stale-rootedness … words without space
or life or liveliness

Without room around the words
without words that leave the reader room-   [room/room-to-grow/grow]
    to-grow and reach around the poet's thoughts
      there is no poem worthy of its ink-   [ink/inkling/lingering]
ling-ering in the ephemera like a stagnant
bit of flatulence

Inspiration floats in and out of my mind
but the poem is more than just its opening thrust-   [thrust/thrust-fault/fault]
    fault of compressed ideas, one usurping another
      one without grace or ease-   [ease/easily/silly]
silly ideas crush over each other when pushed
not spun gossamer

You see, the poem is the thing
not the idea, as beauty emanates on-   [on/only/lyrical]
    ly-rical wings that the poet creates
      within the poem and past the idea-   [idea/ideally/lyrically]
ly-rically, elegiacally, alluringly collection
of simply words

The idea disappears in this good song
as beauty prevails, whether the po-em-   *[poem/path/empathy]*
      path-y laden, ugliness tainted
        cruel, kind, forsaken, love-laced-   *[love-laced/love-laced-up/laced-up]*
up neatly and logically, or loose, free and fluttering
captures your imagination

In the tube
(or M.y R.ecurrent I.maginings)
(June 21, 2009)

Where do I find consolation for my mind's eye
    as I lie flat-backed in the narrowing lumen
Illumine my inner vision, O God, pray I
    as the electric hammers pulse and pound amen

Wandering visage of Elysian pastures
    meandering thoughts of poetic stanzas and verse
Blessed distraction from diagnostic immure
    magnetic detachment from prognosis as worse

Worsening, wandering, willingly waiting
    grinding to what, as I lie in my chamber
    be gone from me, mind, fearful thoughts ruminating
Give to me, God, the most beautiful timbre
    propel mine eye forward with musical mission
    "Come Holy Ghost*" sings to make mind's revision

Thomas Tallis' Ordinal

I think I'll write a new poem …
(June 22, 2009)

Just a shitty day

Actually, don't feel inspired
        enough to do
        so … better to start a
        new

day tomorrow … baked tuna
        sandwiches can
        only
        help!

maybe a little dill pickle in the
        mix then … and
        something poetic
        will come

TDTTTD
(Theresa Daly Therapeutic Touch ..)
(June 27, 2009)

Some people ask or wonder or perhaps
        just need me to tell them what has been a gift
        in this strange and awful journey

Many are reluctant to address the question, as
        fear rises when opening the lid on the possibility
        of something good coming out of hell

But life is never all one or the other
        never all good or all bad
        usually some oscillating mixture
        nearer the middle

I saw a poem of mine recently about "stress" from
        four years ago; about what stress I cannot presently recall
        and of course, in my new crash-course-come-doctorate
        I recognize that I did not know stress then
        (which does not mean I didn't experience distress
        of some degree now and then)

Our life is now stress-filled, with the unending battle against
        the disease
        the cost of the battle, in sheer prostration, fatigue of fatigue,
        soul-numbing hospitalization, recurrence of tumour and vigorous
        blossoming of cancerous cells in unwanted locations,
        fear of the unknown next – of widowhood – of telling our children
            (though we have always kept them in the loop)
            the possible awful truth at some point
                deep dread of that particular conversation

So it is that we still oscillate, closer to the bad end of the
        qualitative spectrum, whatever the hell that is
        but we are not trapped in despair, nor pessimism

and we laugh, revel in life's silly moments,
kiss our children vigorously, but not desperately
and we live the moments inbetween
where life is
and the little gifts arise
But if you were to ask me of one gift in particular
and I have received many, whether tangible or subtle
I would immediately and directly tell you of this strange
and elusive and substantial gift called
therapeutic touch
(which it is)

I have two practitioners who have offered this gift strings-unattached
one since the beginning of my hell
and one for more than a year as well

They come at different parts of my week and offer their time
and grace and art of healing un-touch
And here is where words, as often, come to the precipice
of uselessness …

How do I, a man of science and letters and principles
high-minded and proud
(or once proud, to tell the truth, as malignancy makes level
the playing field of pride)
How do I put into words the sacred and subtle art of what happens
to my "energy field" when I am so expertly practised upon

I do not

Experiences that go beyond words should not be measured in them

---

But a poem without words appears contrived and mischievously composed,
so I will apportion a few observations on TT:
    it is to be cleaned and cleared
        not fixed or healed
    it is to be given gentle direction
        rather than propelled in a correct way
    it is to be given the opportunity to really truly relax
        rather than conjuring some false idle place that lacks reality
    it is to be offered a more natural flow to whatever it is that is one's energy
        not something new or grand or life-changing

It is grounding and familiar and consoling and for me
    helps to re-jig the sway that creeps insidiously in from disease

TT smoothes the flow to my betterment
    away from cancer chaos
        especially that level below my consciousness

And so I preach the gospel of this gift:
    do not forgo the healing hand, the therapeutic un-touch
    do not underestimate the power of its simplicity
    especially in the face of the complex, harrowing nature of
        other treatments

When humbled beyond your darkest imaginings of humility
    be open to a touch therapeutic
    eschew pride and accept a gift
        there is no other way to navigate this journey

Dappled Day's End
(June 27, 2009)

Consider stippled streaming at day's end
along the line of sky's unending limb
as dusk unfolds with plunging bid of sin
to carry forth the wages past the bend

But day breaks clean to rest in sparkling black
which wipes the bloody-rood from memory's sight
So is the deepest cover of good night
to smother over colour on day's back

And mother pray to you for your son's way
as dew descends to freshen birthing morn
New day ascends with promise, not forlorn
though shadow lengthens with the hours' decay

For freshness comes with bitterness in hand
Life ushers forth eschewing all tinged bland

Some words are not for poetry

a set of 3 poems

Some words are not for poetry - I
(July 2, 2009)

Some words are not inherently poetic
    not naturally intended for poetry
    so they shouldn't be used

For instance, words that are clinical, anatomical
    like corpuscular and scrofular and testicular
    onomatopoeically pustular and overly muscular
    but surely not poetical particulars

Though I do recall my grandfather always wheezily laughing
    as he drove us by the sign for Ball's Falls nature reserve
    "It's real name is Testicular Torrents" he would heightenedly whisper

Testicular torrents has wonderful poetic flow to it
    besticular water falls we'd ever seen
    though early spring the air was filled with
    the most pesticular bugs to taint the scene

Perhaps I'm wrong, it's not clinical terms, but
    surely some classes of words just don't work
    long, complicated, antiquated words
    like onomatopoeia could never be used in a poem
    they are too onomatopoetically obstructive to the cadence and verse

No, I'm still barking up the wrong tree here
    what about overly familiar phrases and clichés
    acting as minimizers of poetic intent, blocking the
    circulation of inspiration
and we all know that an ounce of inspiration is worth a pound
    of perspiration

Am I just chasing my tale of poetic woe in this?
    is there a case for prescribing poetic delimits
    (perhaps over-alliterative delimit delineation should be determined and
    possibly discredited)

"Hey, that's out-of-bounds, your poem is disqualified
from the firmament"

In the end, of course, there is no boundary to the wealth of poetic
    words and images
    thank God
    but I would pose a caveat (a non-cavitating one at that)

My concern is ugliness
    not the exploration of such for poetic purpose
    nor the need for all poetry to be beautiful
    but rather the objective of ugliness for its own sake
    whether salacious, violent, abusive, degrading to spirit
    exploitive, harmful, absolutely non-edifying
    and sadly, as a bottom line, evil

I decry the poem that espouses this ugliness, in all its
    guises, manipulative masks, its sheer ugliness
We poets cannot tolerate ugliness as an object and we must
    reject evil as a place of poetic residence, though not as part
    of a cadenced, explorative journey

Poetry is about beauty, pure and complicated
    the unfolding of a flower
    the rebirth of a dormant idea
    the retelling of tragedy to Shakespearean intent
    the revealing of personal scars which give access to the ineffable

Some words are not for poetry – II
(August 18, 2009)

If some words are not good
    for poetry
and yet I have proved this
    wrong, then
though poetry is for the
    true exploration and
    expression of beauty
beauty in all its shades,
    guises

Some paths to beauty may
    traverse ugliness, even
    an edge of sinister intent

So was my face, as little
    as some years ago
not necessarily a place
    of settled beauty
but nonetheless placed
    calmly, proper composed,
    as symmetrical as
    nature intended

I was content and comfortable
    with that visage
    continuous with the
    oldest memories I
    have of my self

Now strange and disturbing
    devolution, devolvement
    down from my
    diseased eye

Sheer ugliness, which I cannot face
    or tolerate, stomach, condone

Is there a face to this with
    any beauty possible? Is
    there merit to poetic
    expression of this
    tumourous torture
    (of mine)

I keep it patched and
    clean and neutral
    though in no possible way
    beautiful

And when I change the
    dressing, I cringe and
    shudder and shut eye
    as best I can

Light floods through
    the murky mess and
    hurts, messing my
    mind's eye as well

There is nothing well to
    this, and yet here
    I ponder beauty

How?

Well, here is the gift
    worth expressing
Beauty emanates from
    mind's eye, and I
    can distance myself
    from the ugliness

Even free my eye,
    mine I,
    to a new beauty
    not before explored
    gift from diseased mire
    bestow, inspire

Some words are not for poetry - III
(September 19, 2009)

Onomatopoetically sung song
spun beauty as gossamer thread glistening
I slide down dew-laced air always listening
to words tinged with heaven's grace, but strung strong

Love does come to me, spinning and bathing
clothing and cradling my soul in its care
Beauty arises with silk gauze my wear
dressing, caressing, nudged gently wading

Into deep pondering life-weaving in awe
of wonder, surrender to beauty's great
latticework frame, which cloaks and sustains us
translucent, hushed humbly, naked and raw
Into this beauty we spin without weight
hosanna-hymn laced with wild gentleness

Bag-of-bones

(August 6, 2009)

Bag-of-bones
sinewed shafts of trabecular lengths
hollows where muscles once stood
long-standing too, they were,
hewn from years of building up
now hollowed out limbs and trunks
fleshless
roughened with vessels prominent through papery skin
and rolled together with tendinous bits poking
along the long skinny lengths

Once a decently sized tall man of fine strength
now my effort channelled into strength of character
rather than body
muscles that snapped to attention and did my bidding
without a doubt
now lie dormant, vacated by instinct and innervation
lacking all welfare
to maintain and compose the wholeness of
the body

Necessarily visiting the tensions
between my physical self and the other side
living a disconnect between the corporeal and psychological
revisiting the great Cartesian dichotomy
dilemma of mind-body divide:
where do I stand
or fall as the case may be?

"I atrophy, therefore I am":
as the body disassembles, disentangles, diseases
the mind seems clear
save the occasional morphine

"I am distracted by disassembly, therefore I am":
as the body contracts, constricts, contorts
the mind clouds with pain, anxiety and lack of abatement
it seems one package, undivided, undividable

And yet at times the mind engages independently
even briefly
even opiate-laced (perhaps because)
and walks freely amongst the bones that pile,
freed of any tether, ligament unbound
and a synapse of thought or poetic phrase or vein of musical impulse
arises, circulates
freely and vitally

Let me be clear here
this is no place for ten syllables of fourteen lines
for linear structure of expression
this is sheer freedom for what is utter existence:

"The mind rests free in the midst of gravity's bonds on the body's bones"

This unforgiving bond-on-bones cannot grasp, clasp the mind's reach:
beyond the body's tethers, its frailties, its sufferings
the mind can and will
move past
any physical misgiving
through the bag-of-bones
and into a orbit of elegance, angularity, truthfulness, vitality

"Cogito, ergo sum":
is enough of a reason
is, in fact, the reason
to persevere despite the bag-of-bones

The mind contributes independently of the body
and then beyond

it is the soul of very existence
allowing navigation through the bones
and then beyond the bones as they turn to dust

As I hollow further and my trunk shrivels in strength
(not that I aspire to decrepitude)
as my limbs further wither and desquamate
leaving sinewy bones and wasted spaces
under what was once a healthy canopy
firmly rooted, solid, connecting earth toward heaven

I gain consolation in the mind's eye, vision free of constitution
living in the canopy green and fertile, strange and imagining
clear and autonomous, mobile and life-blooded
virile and eternal, giver of hope and bestower of the necessary will
to step tenderly over the bag-of-bones
tiptoe through the trabeculations
negotiate past the hollowing, harrowing trunk

As the physical falls away, as it always does
for all living things
the mind, my mind, breeds new life
permeated with life-blooded-sap
impervious to disease
never to be subsumed by my
bag-of-bones

Mary Oliver Set

Thirteenth Moon
(August 8, 2009)

I love her poetry, even adore it.
She has a luxuriant simplicity to her expression –
not that she is ever shallow or simple or transparent –
as she immerses herself in the natural world,
all its bounty and beauty, its tragedy and clarity.

Today I read from *Twelve Moons* while in the bath,
the bath a relatively rare occasion for me, and
reading in the bath something even rarer.
And I read of her immersion in the pink-mooned pond,
her transformation into the joyful singing frog, just
birthed into the April night with its choir of compatriots.

I marvelled at the experience of her chrysalis-tic movement
from budding frog in the cold chains of the black water
back to female-form turning to mud and leaves, turning
like a lonely spindle in the moonlight,
saying "yes".

But this is not my experience of nature, nor
should it be. She has an immediacy that eludes me, and I
think makes me ever so jealous –
though I do not tend toward jealousy.

Her experience is so total and participatory and exquisite.
I just wonder at it, what it must be like. For I sit more on
nature's periphery, easy to self-observe
when on the shore of my life's lake presently, though the
rain drizzles through this intemperate day – poorly temperated too!

Huron roles out from my vision, massive and unending against the
lake-coloured sky, the hue of drizzled water shaded by grey crayola
from shore to horizon and oscillating back in the firmament.

Nature for me is vast and more connected to the grandeur of Hopkins, and yet the little, daily, cyclical observations she makes are alluring, though not mine. I have lain under my childhood sky, azure-deep, and contemplated the magnificence of the rapidly cascading clouds.

But I have not had the experience of missing any chance to swerve past the black snake flashing across the road in an instant, now lifeless, the old bicycle tire, providing rare insight into death, one of nature's absolutes.

I am a keen observer of matters deadly, but the black snake's sudden demise doesn't lend me her gift. Her immersion, baptism in the pink-mooned (and I'm sure) inky-black pond, her transformation from froglet to re-emergent, reborn woman, is singularly beautiful, and yet I am not of that experience.

I quest to swim into Huron's magnificence, beyond my abilities, to the purity of its green-blue and to that perfect of summer days – no crayola gray drizzle, nor invisible horizon. I have been there some years ago, where the water and air match in warmth, and the day feels limitless.

In that day, by myself, I would immerse and remain in the great lake's vast ampleness, float until the need for existence dissipates, gaze round at unending waves of luxuriant lapping against my unnecessary body, and release myself to go with the black snake, who happened upon her unswerving road only to be carried quiet as a dead brother and cool as braided whip into the nearby bushes.

from *Twelve Moons* by Mary Oliver:
"Pink Moon – The Pond"
"The Black Snake"

from Gerard Manley Hopkins:
"God's Grandeur"

A Fourteenth Moon?
(August 11, 2009)

Perhaps I was wrong in considering myself not interested in
nature's minutiae.
She, of course, is a glorious observer of the small things in
our natural world, and I would not place
myself in her league of inherent observance.

But I recalled, after leaning towards Hopkins the other day, my
seminal encounter with the dying sparrow. Returning home after
school, teenaged, alone in the quiet house – not quite so quiet as it
should have been, for there was an odd, flapping, anxious noise in
my sister's room.

The bird had entered through the fireplace and then encountered
our cat, a certain killer. She was chest-heaving and broken-winged and
fatally damaged, simply scrambling for a bit of prolonged existence.

Lovely grey and blue plumage, flurry of feathers, beautifully stained with
dark splotches of red, blood a flowing testimony of her death-writ.

Written in nature's own hand, I the executioner, sparrow the condemned.

Never my role, no farm boy history, no inclination to killing living things
for entertainment. What to do? No reference to the dapple-dawn-drawn
dauphin of Hopkin's sublime envy – no reference to
any grandiosity of nature's being. There is ugly work to be done
at my hand.

Pride and plume pushed into paperbag, I cannot recall how exactly. Some
movement, but generally still, perhaps settled with confinement and the
inability to fight any further. Hemorrhaging-stained brown paper, bowels-strained,
final stress in the bird's life story. Bloody-fecal parchment lending no
poetic colour to the situation.

Out to the back garden, source of freedom, though now differently purposed. Flat, sharp, steel shovel, not for dismemberment, but one crushing blow – quickly, purposely, decisively and done.

I recall the yard as deathly quiet, but for all I knew the trees and telephone wires were filled with sparrows, onlookers in the execution, respecters of nature's way. I plead innocent to her death, and never looked into the obliterated bag – just dug the hole, placed it in, deeply, and covered her up.

Back into the house, young-man-warrior, tears streaming down peach-fuzzed face, no resolution for my novice soul.

A call to beloved grandfather, whose wisdom claimed the necessity of ugly acts at special times, like this, ending the sparrow's suffering. And then it struck me, nature's little synchronicity:

> *God sees the little sparrow fall,*
> *it meets His tender view.*
> *If God so loved the little bird,*
> *I know he loves me too.*

Hymn of my childhood, solace perfectly placed. And today I again see the poetic salvation in the bird's tragedy. It is not Hopkin's grandeur, soaring chevalier, master of the sky. It is again her (not the sparrow), gifted observer of nature on any scale.

I am, sadly, dangerous entering the kingdom of the sparrow. Though I would dream to lie about and witness nature's glory, soaring story of sparrows and crows and finches and starlings, they would know me for what I am.

And I should go, no true dreamer or eater of leaves, rather reluctant executioner, lover of the fallen bird. But, yes my dear, the blue-bleak-beaked embers do fall, gall themselves, and gash gold-vermillion – even beauty arises on paperbags.

> from *Twelve Moons* by Mary Oliver: "Entering the Kingdom"
> from Gerard Manley Hopkins: "The Windhover"

Dream Moon – Smell of Rain and Last Soliloquy
(August 12, 2009)

Do you know the smell?
She does, going into the woods when the rain is over, the
path a swamp, the trees freshly dripping. That unmistakable
smell of nature's watershower permeating cedar boughs, mossy soil, sopping
bark and rotting wood.

I love the smell, especially in the season of my heart's delight, as orange-burnt
leaves change from brightly brittle to mushy compost, only adding further
pungency to the odour after rainfall. Earthy, musky smell, redolent of
old red wine kept too long in a musty cellar, still remembering harvest-ripe
fruit, but now rich and inky and ever so stinky, though not in any
unpleasant manner.

Swollen creeks driven with mud and ambitions, push us on to dreams in this
lusty, musty atmosphere – nature sopping with secrets, saturated with little
soliloquies. Creeks that poured smoothly only last week, now flush with
life and mess and rain's overburden. Overburgeoning banks swell with thick
silt, platted leaves and rain's smell of fresh detritus, attractive to the primordial
nose and spurring to the mind.

Last week the creeks sang with bird voices, and now they are crazed with the
steeping and glutting of rain – bubbling smell of flooded forest, fragrant leaf-mould
and luscious loamy muck. Skyless moonlight shines on mud's lustrous wetness.

She writes of great dreams in this humid headspace, where her two uncles once
went west full of hope and vision. But just as nature promises rebirth in
this fertile, permeating ground, so it also conjures death, around the
corner, the bend where dreams curve to an end.

They became rich as their dreams and healthy as animals, she recalls, but also
eventually turned the corner in humus-healed boots, and became two graves
under the leaves – where dreams permanently rest with boots pointed up to
waterlogged clouds and the mind meandering in the murky mess of
nature's wet and sweetly-perfumed sweepings.

from *Twelve Moons* by Mary Oliver: "Dreams"

Of Importance
(August 12, 2009)

The other day, actually it was this evening, I realized that I am terribly important
    terrifically important – honestly –
    just like you and all the others
I was watching an old episode of the West Wing
    nobly-principled president of my perfect dream
    making my mind expansive
    bigger than life
There he stood, kindling reelection at some military base in Indiana
    rousing my moral idealism and fictional patriotism while a massive flag
    hovered unfurled in the background

And suddenly it dawned on me: all those past invitations and conclaves
    made retrospective sense because of my newly realized importance –
    my meeting with the prime minister, and all the others,
    and with the president and also various dictators
My meeting, some years ago, with the pope at a lovely little café in Florence
    the archbishop with tea and then after the hours passed
    some Scotch slowly sipped
    and all the various cardinals and bishops and deacons over many years

The Dalai Lama called some years ago, he is a voice-to-voice kind of man
    but the date he proposed conflicted with my appointment with
    Nelson Mandela, which was to be Winnie-free and at his weekend
    retreat outside Johannesberg
So Mandela won out over any mandala at the time, and the Dalai and I could
    never sync our calendars
Letterman called once, yes he himself, and then begged off as wrong number
    when he found out I was Canadian... something about "quota met"
    but I think he and Paul may have been having a rough phase at the time

Oprah's team called twice, but their conditions were strange, and perhaps
    my importance was intimidating for her, too mano-a-mano
Various think-tanks and intellectuals and celebrities have contacted me for

advice, sometimes well under the radar, which is fine
I've never been attracted to the publicity, but it is finally nice to understand why
    all the summons and summits through my years:
      the sheer importance of me, well and you, and all the others of course
The intellectuals always have terribly specific questions, inquiries, which
      make for efficient conversation, and given the way my mind
      works, its importance you know, leading to quick and clear answers
John Keynes and something macroeconomic, Vaclav Havel and something
      poetically political, Stephen Hawking and some space-time thing,
      Barack Obama with a specific sartorial subject, Vladimir Horowitz with a
      question of fingering pattern, and Alec Trebek with some incidence of
      great jeopardy
Make no mistake, there have been great women as well: Mother Theresa with a
      quiet matter, Katherine Hepburn with some fascinating questions about
      blocking. Yoko Ono with many questions of why, Nigella Lawson with
      many questions that I couldn't answer (or deemed wise not to do so),
      Jackie Kay really just for a chat, and Anne Hathaway, well actually, I
      phoned her

Of course part of being important is an inflationary sense of self which goes well
      beyond the magnitude of one's actual importance
I was just discussing this with Jimmy Carter the other day, or
      was it Bono?
Anyway, when you deflate the falsely inflated part of yourself, all the heated
      expansive importance, you are left, shockingly, with
      your real self

So sadly I and all the dignitaries and luminaries I have referenced are, under
      the skin of it, rubber-balloon-walled skin, are just the same
      in terms of importance

Ego be damned! The human condition calls us to sameness in humility, when
      stripped past our skin, all it's rubbery layers, some thick, some thin
Down to the basics, naked, wasted, fragile, we are the same creatures, further
      DNA-evidenced, but enough proven in our humble existences, if

we allow ourselves the luxury of truth in self(less)-examination
Flesh and bone, mind and soul basics

Though, I must say, the importance was nice while it lasted, and all the meetings,
    caucuses, political and religious trysts were, well, exciting, in
    hindsight, and quite terribly important

My Camera
for Larry
(August 17, 2009)

I remember an old friend
    he of the perfectly placed
    occasional outlandish
    statement,
commenting upon his lack of
    camera on our tour

Of course we all had cameras,
    with film no less,
    to capture our snapshots
    south from England up to Scotland

The cathedrals we sang in
    the timbre-thatched
    cobble streets we
    whittled our way through

Punting on the River Cam
tracing our way round
    York's Roman walls
roaming around
    speckled Scottish fishing villages
cobbling our path up Arthur's
    Seat behind our
    residence in Edinburgh

Yet he never proclaimed
    need of camera nor
    bemoaned any lack
    of Kodak
"My camera is in my
    head" and we
    laughed, knowing better

And yet he was always
        so contented and engaged
        with our touring, never
        a complaint

Now I think of a different
        day, much different,
        and closer to home
        and heart
She will play Beethoven
        this afternoon with the
        faculty string quartet

And I pondered the camera
        or camcorder, all digitized
        and slick and unobtrusive
        in hand
But I have decided not to
        view her performance
from any other lens than
        my own

"My camera is in my
        head", clear and
        focused, high
        definition with full
        zoom capability …
        in the instant of a
        synaptic snapshot

Filming on the back of
        my brain, perhaps an
        outlandish statement,
        but recorded in truth,
Mind reeling, rolling
        with our reality through
        my only real viewpoint

Au Revoir Aubade

(August 17, 2009)

I have been asked to write an Aubade
    poem's short night two lovers have had

Long night comes short with lark's dawning cry
    'tis morning or mourning brings lark's call to die?

Juliet cries nightingale not lark
    sun's exhalation douses the dark

Put me to death pleads grey Romeo
    'tis not day yet, pray speak of the soul

Yet straining discord the lark does make
    harsh morning's dawn on fresh love doth break

Farewell, Aubade, au revoir sin's lark
    death imparts its blow, light fades to dark

Lovers' pleas extinguished with lark's call
    end of love's time, farewell, adieu all

reference: Act III, Scene 5
The Tragedy of Romeo and Juliet
by William Shakespeare

Girl with the flower

(August 30, 2009)

"Et incarnatus est de Spiritu Sancto ex Maria Virgine, et homo factus est"

I

Incarnation, the word is
    poetry itself
not the image of Renaissance repose
    with tall multi-stemmed lily in hand
not that Botticelli's Cestello painting isn't
    exquisite
nor that the vestal, openly-ovular, stamen-
    studded flower isn't vividly
    serenely symbolic
but it is anachronistic artistry
    far-removed from the earthy
    palette of annunciation
so I will paint with words, not
    multi-hued oil paste

There is a moment of convergence between
    his painting and mine, where
celestial light emanates from unseen source in the ordered room
    (though I envision her outside in an olive grove
    at the time of the angel's intercession)

She of swarthy complexion, too young
    for the wisdom necessary
hard-working peasant hands stained
    with black olives
chipped fingers by dry stone and
    arid, fertile soil
lustrous dark wild hair
but deep, pensive, pure eyes

She could always say no to the offer
        Offer? Decree? Command? Announcement?
Angelic presence not calming nor soothing, could
        a mere mortal actually decline?

Could she actually accept such a life-changing
        culture-contravening, audacious venture?

Yet she kneels down on bruised knee
        lies flat before the angel
        perhaps seeing the grave
        danger in acceptance
the futility of 33 years' gestation
        the foreshadowing of darkness
        and light (now filtering
        flickering through olive trees'
        verdant canopy)

She accepts, accedes, even acquiesces
she nods, bows, prostrates herself
        no virgin queen, no noble mantle
she opens to incarnation
        to its absurdity and abundance
changes the history of our
        world, our universe

II

The stirrups open to face the door
but the clinic physician always sits with her stool
        just poised to block any unannounced entry

She is but fourteen, convinced by a friend to get
        tested
already an abortion, too many "partners" and
        scars, mars from risks better unmentioned

she timid and yet tattooed
      coy and precocious

The broom-closet-room lit only with one
      block of fluorescents
small sink in a corner and a few
      bare cupboards
window permanently covered with
      dust-impregnated blinds

She is pretty, underneath the make-up and
      persistent anxiety
too familiar with the guidance counsellors
      for her wayward marks
chipped split black-painted fingernails
      chewed on
dark smudged hands from mascara accidents
her hair two-toned, ironed straight
      wildly frizzed when slightly humid
but deep, pensive, pure eyes

The angel arrives now as she awaits
      any purpose in life
      incarnation's poetry, volatile gift for damaged
child, now heaven's woman of grace
reborn virgin of modern era
      bearer of history's second Messianic gift, breaking
      time and expectation
A new Saviour for our time?

Will she accept? Acquiesce to the offer?
Can she recognize the moment of
      intercession and slide off the table
      onto the floor in humility and reverence?
Will anyone burst in? Does she have
      time to pull her gown together
      before the angelic presence?

She is overwhelmed, unsure, only having
hoped for The Pill
as sole prescription for her day

And now the angel presents her
with the tall unbridled lily
graceful, simple, pure
symbol through time
and the room's light has transformed
as if the blinds are opened
and the moon and sun have together
filtered down dappled light
upon His chosen servant

III

The gilding off bright lily's petals white
she flowers, up right as symbol 'gainst man's fall
her sinless nature marked with heavenly call
she acquiesces altering human plight

Voluptuous lily stamen blazing bright
stands tall, erect and proud above the gall
conception's carpel blossoms clear and all
rests elegantly brushed by holy light

Womb flushed with Spirit's touch, word incarnate
bud bulging fleshed out on green flowering shoot
acceded deed, now nature's gravid path

Luminous corolla in unlaced state
verdant calyx unlocks stigmata's root
lifts angel, lily's bloom fleshed by heaven's breath

with appreciation for the Madonna lily paintings by:
Sandro Botticelli
Leonardo da Vinci
Bartolomé Esteban Perez Murillo
Eustache Le Sueur
Francesco Albani

with appreciation for the inspiration of:
"Annunciation" by Denise Levertov

Kris poems

a set of 3 poems for Maggie and Howard

Child of God
(September 1, 2009, for Howard & Maggie)

Ah, child of God – my child
      how does it come to this?
You now fetalized, needing rebirth
      lying beautifully in repose, restful, away
      from us in some place, we pray,
      of utter peace

But you must come back
      we need you, child
Your child needs you
      this is not your time
      or ours, for departures, farewells or
      any such social graces

You lie gracefully, hair back and lustrous
      like your quiet lips
Spit out the tube and sit up and let's have
      one of our good old chats

For I need one now, my child,
      you seem too remote and
      I don't like it
      not one bit

Come back, beloved, to the
      land of all your loved ones,
      my child,
Let go of your place in heaven
      just for now
      for we need you, here

You have been bathed today, tubes and wires and all
      and yet we bathe you in our love continually
      in the community of prayer

in the single purpose of bringing you
back to us

Child of God, come bathe with us in the
    crisp Autumn light, lengthening shadows and
    life-affirming colours – can you smell the brisk air?

We await you, our dearest one

She is your daughter
(September 4, 2009, for Howard & Maggie)

> *"O Lord, give thy Holy Spirit into our hearts, and lighten*
> *our understanding, that we may dwell in the fear of thy Name"*

She is your daughter –
    my sister –
        your mother –

She of unnecessary fragile state, un-right place
    wrong of time and space
    yet calm, elegiac face
façade of acceptance, consent it appears

Tubes with wires, mechanical means, and our tears
    fears of the possible, unutterable, terrible
tragedy not to be embraced, but damnable!

How to intervene, intercede, even substitute one's self
    to coerce, cajole, constrain her to regaining, retaining herself?

Your son, brothers, mother, father call you forth, back to homing
    come out of your coma, your away-dome, your gloaming
    get up from your I.C.U. catafalque, cataclysm, cruciforming
    and stop this most heaven-ward randomly roaming

We do, though, reluctantly cease our demands – daughter, sister, mother,
    and transform into prayer, our pleas, intercessing together

Please, Lord, we cry, give us back your frail servant
    if You may, if You can, if our frangible, tangibly-chafed world allows, fervent
    we pray, You may – wholly, holy insistent we stay
human affliction, tribulation, now our constant, continuous foray

We beseech, O Lord, if she is to go beyond this façade
    that you accept her with indefinite love, tenderness, then
    we'll promenade
    mournfully, through our backyard, the churchyard and graveyard
and yet communally we will celebrate her life, vital spirit
    (but damn our assent, any blessing, great spit –
    what if she now unexpectedly aspirate?)

Expectorate that tube, daughter-sister-mother sweet-
    one – we call out to you, from the dim-deep, your heartbeat
    continues to pound in our breasts, no retreat, none defeat
We unceasingly, increasingly cry out to God bittersweet
    that over your placid, cool face, draped, no sheet
    shall rest, as your death is swallowed up, full and complete

Into the woods
(September 8, 2009, for Howard & Maggie)

"You are indeed nestled thickly in the woods, but what an alive and wild place
the forest can be ... dangerous, but real, filled with life!
This is a good place, even if tempered with anxiety."

Into the woods we will walk, we will go
    where it will take us, nobody knows

Into the wild of the lush forest cloak
    we will follow the leaf trail, ashes and smoke

Into the smoke of the burnt umber leaves
    where the fronds waif in the smouldering breeze

There we will pause, in the midst of still wood
    where clear we will hear of all that is good

It is good in the woods where the people do gather
    we should linger here now, before we scram and scatter

And bask in the redolent crisp Autumn air
    where the world is alive with a scent all too spare

Into wildness, scorched orange sienna black-green
    enveloping branches of creatures unseen

Into, around us, we are not out-of-the-woods
    there are risks, perhaps damage to some of our goods

Good God, take us deep into forest's dark bower
    before we step back for the sake of the hour

Deep into the woods, we will nestle and rest
    where life abides verdantly with earthy warm breast

Past the smoke of the moss on our feet, past the mire
      we will stomp out the ashes, pour out the fire

The wild wood gives us life, bogged with uncertainty
      where it goes, no one knows – the path pied, lichens, scree

We are free in the breeze and the muck and the trees
      Lord, take us deep past the smoke-crackling leaves

Coat us with wild caress, renewal and grace
      green us with life and the hushed peace of this place

Old poems sit
(September 5, 2009)

Old poems sit in my journal collecting dust
  some are quite fine, others just so

They are mine, no doubt, me then
  connecting to them, then sometimes an odd task

Then to now, my voice disconnected
  though recognized, sans sense of continuity

I am thankful for this old voice
  therapeutic in a way

"Buxtehude Blues" at midnight some years ago
  yes, I remember, that's me!

Gone is my boyhood
(September 6, 2009)

Gone is my boyhooded morning erection
　　　　now is the thrusting of dawn's insurrection

Pulling together my cells, mind and body
　　　　sorting this bag-of-bones, groping all shoddy

Should I get up, does it matter on whole?
　　　　Given the damage rests hard on my soul

Hard I lie, buttock gone, stiff as a board
　　　　get me up, standing straight, point up toward

Neutropenic anemia, lack of blood's flow
　　　　lift me and prick me and rouse me to go

Ah, bed's soft comfort, flaccidly pleasant
　　　　why rise up impotent, downy lair's pheasant?

Power does dissipate, dilapidating
　　　　never flush, nor tumesced, limpid pulsating

Wake-up call in morning's blown nested down
　　　　leaving erection's prod nudging around

Stanched resurrection comes rigid by force
　　　　my love's plea to rise up just chaste intercourse

Enough to convince me – breakfast's tastiest pleasure
　　　　erection absence moot, toasty egg's pastry measure!

Bloody Hell
(September 17, 2009)

Whacked with closing cupboard door against my deteriorating face – bloody
hell it hurt; but alas my right-sided neglect, caught in an innocent instant

Sitting in the study, recomposed, little weepage from my eye, normal
not when ruddy smear all over my hand from wiping – bloody
mess, bleary bloody hell all over

Back to the bathroom and – hell – pooling, weeping bloody mess under the
dressing, matting and gnarling up the poultice, red mess of
hemorrhage welling up visibly underneath

Hell – sheer stress – bloody

Sit down, breathe slow, and pressure on the spot and pressure, she should be
home any moment
any moment

And she is – hell – thank God

Quickly stripped of the crimson dressing and any vestige of composure on my part
more pressure and stop the oozing, nothing arterial – bloody
hell – moment not sanguine, but terribly sanguinous

Within five minutes, I am coagulated, patched, soothed and wonted, whatever
the bloody hell that is

New dressing, new technique, new friability of tissue being treated again and
again and again – bloody hell – with always that corpuscle of hope for
measure gained, a clean clot of stability, just a little while, a
small quest for normalcy, and move away from morbidity, mortality,
zombie-ness … a little sense of the past, but a larger piece of some
un-phlebotomized future

Then, of course, she another she, she my other she
announces her Hallowe'en costume idea that evening –
she and her pack of friends will be
"zombie-rock-stars"
(whatever the bloody hell those are)

And I realize, of course, why not? She has the perfect zombie-model: living, laying,
lying around, oozing here and there, confusing night and day, sloppy-slippery
sanguinary seepage from his two-faced existence

Bloody Hell!

Sonnet's Sonnet
(September 19, 2009)

> *"So long as men can breathe or eyes can see,*
> *So long lives this and this gives life to thee."*

Creating sonnets is not terr'bly hard.
Iambic feet give pulse to poem's song.
Italian form or English like the Bard –
yield rhyming structure ten syllabic long.

Aside from this there's little more to say:
ABAB – CDCD to start;
pentameter da-DA leaves room for play;
the octave's done its eight line op'ning part.

Now sestet's mood does change with new design,
as rhyming moves to finish up couplet:
fresh thought in poem's scheme t'wards final line.
For Shakespeare's muse we owe the largest debt –
those darling buds of May have borne bright flow'rs
of endless summer's rosy flooded-bowers.

reference: Shakespeare Sonnet XVIII

Rhyming Resolution
(September 23, 2009)

I've resolved to write a poem in rhyme
where senseless message is clear by design
the verse may be curse to poem's good sense
but perhaps some editor with eighty-odd cents

May throw my way a proverbial bone
for penning a poem inanely drone
I don't care, for it's my wish and delight
to wax poetical – quietly slight, quite trite

Pentameter almost, iambic no-no
though here a "da-Da" stanza, just below:

Your <u>need</u> for <u>metric structure raised</u> as <u>moot</u>
when <u>rhyming pattern makes</u> no <u>useful fit</u>
so <u>look</u> to <u>entertainment in</u> the <u>foot</u>
of <u>doggerel</u> verse <u>silly</u>-<u>slippery shit</u>

Do watch your slide through stench of crafty go-go
before you know, poem will reach out to bestow

Artful (sinful) craft on cranium's halo
where couplets undergo relief surrender
to digestive push of alternating flow
with rhyming opposite lines so verse comes tender

And not be circumspect of structure's rigor
when composition is an act of vigor
and poesy end-stops when could end-jamb up-
upon the mountain ecstasy's erupt-

Tion, shown, blown, thrown strewn down the gauntlet stone
past arched romantic ode, semi-unpedantic toad
when sometimes all we need is chamber's groan:
commodious giggling, emptying pot's fresh load

He spat into dry ground

(September 30, 2009)

He spat into the dryness of the ground,
where the ochred earth sat dim under light:
Spittle makes clay, anointing sightless eyes.

In the muddy poultice clean light is found;
murky haze, rebirth, brings shades not yet bright:
He spat into the dryness of the ground.

Viscous spit hits parched soil scorching fresh wound;
bloody loam smeared onto sinner contrite:
Spittle makes clay, anointing sightless eyes.

Unshod we all stand on tamped earthen bound;
sinner vaguely sees gift through muddened sight:
He spat into the dryness of the ground.

Despite no need for gesture, He cupped round
simple sin of blinded eye, mucking blight:
Spittle makes clay, anointing sightless eyes.

Sent to wash, little man with visage crowned,
not with thorn or nettle, but with clay's bite:
He spat into dry air of boundless skies.
Spittle makes clay, anointing sightless eyes.

> **John 9:6-7 (King James Version)**
> *6 When he had thus spoken, he spat on the ground, and made clay of*
> *the spittle, and he anointed the eyes of the blind man with the clay,*
> *7 And said unto him, Go, wash in the pool of Siloam, (which is by*
> *interpretation, Sent.) He went his way therefore, and washed, and came*
> *seeing.*

John 9 (King James Version)

1 And as Jesus passed by, he saw a man which was blind from his birth.

2 And his disciples asked him, saying, Master, who did sin, this man, or his parents, that he was born blind?

3 Jesus answered, Neither hath this man sinned, nor his parents: but that the works of God should be made manifest in him.

4 I must work the works of him that sent me, while it is day: the night cometh, when no man can work.

5 As long as I am in the world, I am the light of the world.

6 When he had thus spoken, he spat on the ground, and made clay of the spittle, and he anointed the eyes of the blind man with the clay,

7 And said unto him, Go, wash in the pool of Siloam, (which is by interpretation, Sent.) He went his way therefore, and washed, and came seeing.

8 The neighbours therefore, and they which before had seen him that he was blind, said, Is not this he that sat and begged?

9 Some said, This is he: others said, He is like him: but he said, I am he.

10 Therefore said they unto him, How were thine eyes opened?

11 He answered and said, A man that is called Jesus made clay, and anointed mine eyes, and said unto me, Go to the pool of Siloam, and wash: and I went and washed, and I received sight.

12 Then said they unto him, Where is he? He said, I know not.

13 They brought to the Pharisees him that aforetime was blind.

14 And it was the sabbath day when Jesus made the clay, and opened his eyes.

15 Then again the Pharisees also asked him how he had received his sight. He said unto them, He put clay upon mine eyes, and I washed, and do see.

16 Therefore said some of the Pharisees, This man is not of God, because he keepeth not the sabbath day. Others said, How can a man that is a sinner do such miracles? And there was a division among them.

17 They say unto the blind man again, What sayest thou of him, that he hath opened thine eyes? He said, He is a prophet.

18 But the Jews did not believe concerning him, that he had been blind, and received his sight, until they called the parents of him that had received his sight.

19 And they asked them, saying, Is this your son, who ye say was born blind? how then doth he now see?

20 His parents answered them and said, We know that this is our son, and that he was born blind:

21 But by what means he now seeth, we know not; or who hath opened his eyes, we know not: he is of age; ask him: he shall speak for himself.

22 These words spake his parents, because they feared the Jews: for the Jews had agreed already, that if any man did confess that he was Christ, he should be put out of the synagogue.

23 Therefore said his parents, He is of age; ask him.

24 Then again called they the man that was blind, and said unto him, Give God the praise: we know that this man is a sinner.

25 He answered and said, Whether he be a sinner or no, I know not: one thing I know, that, whereas I was blind, now I see.

26 Then said they to him again, What did he to thee? how opened he thine eyes?

27 He answered them, I have told you already, and ye did not hear: wherefore would ye hear it again? will ye also be his disciples?

28 Then they reviled him, and said, Thou art his disciple; but we are Moses' disciples.

29 We know that God spake unto Moses: as for this fellow, we know not from whence he is.

30 The man answered and said unto them, Why herein is a marvellous thing, that ye know not from whence he is, and yet he hath opened mine eyes.

31 Now we know that God heareth not sinners: but if any man be a worshipper of God, and doeth his will, him he heareth.

32 Since the world began was it not heard that any man opened the eyes of one that was born blind.

I am Keats as you are
(October 3, 2009)

I am Keats as you are Keats as you are me and we are all together.
See how they run like cocks from a flock, see how they fly.
I'm dying.

Sitting on a snowflake, waiting for the sled to come.
Operation no wake, stupid bloody sputum,
Man, you been a haughty doc, you let face grow glum.
I am the eggplant, they are the eggplant,
I am the harpseal, goo goo g'joob.

Oncolog'cal doctors shitting
up my life, up your life, without rue.
See how they fly like goosey in the sky, see how they pooh.
I'm crying, I'm dying.
I'm crying, I'm dying.

Yellow matter custard, dripping from my own dead eye.
Craggy-bloody discharge, pornographic kick-ass,
Boy, you been a potty doc you let your ethics pass.
I am the eggplant, you are the eggplant,
I am the harpseal, goo goo g'joob.

Sitting in the rad'ation garden waiting for the burn.
But the glow don't spurn, you get a rash
from sitting on your withering ass.
I am the eggplant, you are the eggplant,
I am the sealharp, goo goo g'joob.

Expert sexpert choking poachers,
don't you know the joker screams at you?
See how they smile like geese in a pie,
see how they fried.
I'm dying.

Sardines in a pickle, huffing up the breathless stairs.
Once a family doctor, singing Bach cantata.
Man, you should have seen me reading Dylan Thomas poems.
I was the eggplant, they were the eggplant,
I am the sealed-heart, goo goo g'joob g'goo goo g'joob.
Goo goo g'joob g'goo goo g'joob g'goo.

I am the walrus – lyrics

(The Beatles: John Lennon, author & lead vocals)

I am he as you are he as you are me and we are all together.
See how they run like pigs from a gun, see how they fly.
I'm crying.

Sitting on a cornflake – waiting for the van to come.
Corporation tea-shirt, stupid bloody tuesday.
Man, you been a naughty boy, you let your face grow long.
I am the eggman, they are the eggmen.
I am the walrus, goo goo g'joob.

Mr. City policeman sitting
Pretty little policemen in a row.
See how they fly like lucy in the sky, see how they run.
I'm crying, i'm crying.
I'm crying, i'm crying.

Yellow matter custard, dripping from a dead dog's eye.
Crabalocker fishwife, pornographic priestess,
Boy, you been a naughty girl you let your knickers down.
I am the eggman, they are the eggmen.
I am the walrus, goo goo g'joob.

Sitting in an English garden waiting for the sun.
If the sun don't come, you get a tan
From standing in the English rain.
I am the eggman, they are the eggmen.
I am the walrus, goo goo g'joob g'goo goo g'joob.

Expert textpert choking smokers,
Don't you think the joker laughs at you?
See how they smile like pigs in a sty,
See how they snied.
I'm crying.

Semolina pilchard, climbing up the Eiffel tower.
Elementary penguin singing Hare Krishna.
Man, you should have seen them kicking Edgar Allan Poe.
I am the eggman, they are the eggmen.
I am the walrus, goo goo g'joob g'goo goo g'joob.
Goo goo g'joob g'goo goo g'joob g'goo.

Let's start at the top
(October 11, 2009)

Let's start at the top with what's left of my mop
the chemo and beam have left a good sheen
a few random hairs sprouting, odd-looking crop
a sense of where eyebrows and lashes have been

Next, to my face, such a strange looking place
one side rather normal, while the other falls off
patched up mucked eye in a state of disgrace
tumourous space, looking tough, sloughed and rough

Boney destruction, lymph nodes unwanted
spots leading nowhere good, dangerously close
disturbing and better-worse, I am undaunted
for I don't look quite as bad as scanning proposes

The purpose of all this? Well, don't get me started
the trial to save my ears lost me my hearing
I virile and active before health departed
now day's strict exercise through sinuses clearing

Mucous my constant companion, my foe
crusties and wheezies, from wherever they come
whether nose, throat or chest, or maybe great toe
middle-night target for coughing chunks of gum

From my lung, back of tongue, now a tradition
sometimes esophagit – is my dilemma
achey back, tender ribs come to fruition
dry skin and rash from drugs scarred erythema

Bloody red, here and there, carves out a niche
ruby-brick, colours-hick, cardinal's bright garment
cracking face, awkward gaze, gory crushed peach
lovely fruit, yet not with devolvement malignant

Back to anatomical survey head-toe
leaving my mind, heart, soul untouched in this
geographical scrutiny of weeping and woe
liver spot newly found, wish it had missed

Missed me entirely, this damned-cancer thing
get thee away from me DNA mutant
not worth the perspective its terror does bring
boney mets everywhere, my fresh pollutant

What is next? As I head below my pelvis
sex life gone thanks to the chemo-radiation
can't grind my hips or I might fracture my Elvis
forgetting my legs in this strange examination

Once I had muscle where buttock should be
bruises and skinny-peg-legs stuck on now
numbed feet and broken nails define lower me
neuropathed hands, how could I forget. Wow!

Am I finished my complaint tirade yet?
Rarely I let it outside so complete
safe here in rhyme meant to defray your fret
my main intent that my heart should still beat

Clearly and crisply to music and poems
up tempo gesture for all of my loved ones
Mary and Theo and Henry – I owe them
debt of my love for their patient endurance

As I the patient kneel bowed down before
the undaunted Presence for whom I adore
as my creator, destructor, magician
heal me, miraculously, O Great Physician!

Autumn's Glance
(October 19, 2009)

Casting a glance past my shoulder as Chopin's Berceuse opens into the air
     light diffuses across the room with its Autumn shadow

     beautiful day … beautiful

     shimmers, ripples as dry, shallow water with dancing shades of
     lilac leaves
     shimmering stream of light across a flaxen silk cushion
     nothing special, but yes
     the glinty lustre lingers here, simple, playful, randomly enticing

My eye to Autumn light is a relationship beyond my strength
     and always has been
     there, an unaccomplished lilac leaf, predominantly green with a touch of
     purplish blush, just flickered down past the window

Magical dance of Autumn's delight, my delight
     the season's progression to detritus and Winter's insulation
     of wilted lamium, hardened rose-hips, flattened hostas

Blankets of leaves form pools of musty colour across our back garden
     (we were all away in different directions this weekend)
     and in this span, the paw-paw simply dropped its voluptuous
     leaves, leaving them strewn in an organized un-windswept circle
     round its barren form

Oh, the motion, waving, blowing, dropping, to barrenness
     who designed this beauty?
     not I, it is beyond my conception
     conceiving barrenness
     nature's movement to senescence

Only she can create such beauty in this strange and entrancing ritual
     Autumn's ebb-and-flow, dappled light, dance of crisp, rufous

leaves, of desiccated, musty, smudged ochre-paper
Little notes tumble through the fresh air and wood-smoke, notes of
truth:

Beauty lives here
Come see and smell and touch
Rusty impregnation of fluttering, flickering light and leaves
preparing for Winter's sleep and Spring's release

Daily Haikus

(September 29, 2009)
A haiku for my day today:

> Highway does not call
> London ceases to exist
> for now, Fall's leaves call

(September 30, 2009)

> Misty London gone
> many little plain tasks beg
> my glad indulgence

(October 1, 2009)
A 5:00 inspiration from the long night:

> Path's way not so clear
> Today darker clouds appear
> Just at bay, my fears

An 11:30 p.m. freer inspiration:

> I watched PBS
> National Parks by Ken Burns
> my mind expansive

(October 2, 2009)
Another 5:00 inspiration:

> Sleep stops five o'clock
> Why? Why not? Another time
> Go now, 4:18

During bone scan, home at 3:00:

> Anywhere comes true
> Everywhere, head-toes, does too
> Messy bed, my head

(October 3, 2009)
The early morning:

> Last's 4:38
> Ha! Quietude and calmness
> No despair this night

(October 4, 2009)
The late night again:

> Ha! I am the farce
> Breathless disquietude hits
> 4:18!! My arse

(October 5, 2009)
5:10 a.m.:

> Discovered gremlin
> uninvited bestower
> sleep's mucous-plugger

7:35 a.m.:

> Spluttering at sink
> Consoling daybreak clearance
> Ah! Prednisone, drowse

(October 6, 2009)
5:18, of all times, just a time-zone shift:

> Gremlin reappears
> Pushing out of my chest wall
> Cough him down the well

(October 7, 2009)
3:43, earlier than usual:

> Gremlin has opened
> A flowering of mucous
> Bud-to-blossoming

(note "bud", not "blood", despite the temptation of a provocative hidden rhyme, alliteration, assonance! … it's just not the case)

(October 8, 2009)
4:19 E.S.T.:

> Ugly wee creature
> He comes at his will, not mine
> I learn to accept

(October 9, 2009)
6:48 a.m., quite late by his "standards":

> Ah! Gremlin, shmemlin
> Oh! You are no never-mind
> To me, I adapt
>
> Your ways cowardly
> Though always most effective
> Expectoration

(October 10, 2009)
At the cottage, 6:48 a.m., which is pretty damn decent:

> This morning's gremlin
> Not such a big deal, unseen
> Shut door cracks – morphine

(October 11, 2009)
After dragging my sorry half-buttock out-of-bed at 11:00 a.m.:

> Sleep's sound night lingers
> Begging indulgent strange dreams
> Kettle chokes, slow poke

(October 12, 2009)
Not really the usual issue:

> Gentle gremlin's nudge
> 6:08 a budge, not dire ...
> ...arrhea comes a flood

(October 13, 2009)
A fine night:

> 6:45 tolls
> the bell, as I shift and roll
> to the toilet bowl

(October 14, 2009)
Anticipating the old route, poor sleep:

> Back through sunny fog
> London reappears, though not
> Emerald city

(October 15, 2009)
After a lovely night of rest:

> Gremlin seems smaller
> These nights come longer, though he
> Knocks softly, calmer

(October 16, 2009)
Tough to bed to begin:

> Tough to begin night's
> Sleep without placid delights
> Insomnia fights

(October 17. 2009)
My love away, but sleep good:

> Strange bed all alone
> Room to spare, but spare the room
> Cat curls up, warm thoughts

(October 18, 2009)
From my day with Laura:

> "TO AUNTIE LAURA"
> Says the bathroom-wall painting
> "LOVE, THEODORA"

(October 19, 2009)
After the lovely weekend and now th'eternal Fall day:

> Unbelievable
> Autumn days fall leavable
> Fallen leaves – bagful

(October 20, 2009)

An uneventful night, coffee starting to stir in me:

> Why daily haiku?
> Have I become addicted?
> Good, simple routine

(October 23, 2009)

Ironically:

> I've lost haiku's thread
> The discipline, daily bread
> Rising yeast, keeps fed

(October 24, 2009)

After a good night's rest:

> Morning comes found blest
> Now to unfold the day's best
> Cottage folds in nest

> Let's resume the thread
> Rise the yeast and bake the bread
> One must eat, be fed

> Thread of discipline
> Voluntary choice made clear
> Routine's benefit

(October 25, 2009)

A frightening night with out-of-control rib pain:

> She tolerates stress
> Even this ungodly hour
> TT hovers peace

Morphine brings relief
But her tenderness transports
flowing calm, love, peace

(October 26, 2009)
A slow, morphine-laced day, but functional:

Go with the flow, man
Catch-up, (moustarde), as you can
Get with it, the plan

Being Completed Elsewhere

Glenn's unfinished symphony

That makes us dream
(begun June 13, 2009)

'Tis music makes us dream
'tis music gives deepest beauty
'tis music that is our clearest connection
      with the Divine
'tis music that creates, is creation, is life

Sit on the edge of my futon
      in the dark
      and listen to Josquin's Agnus Dei
      from his Missa La sol fa re mi
O lamb of God, who giveth music to us
      is it possible not to pray when
      immersed in this sound world?

Come down to my 1970s paneled basement bedroom
      and I will turn up the volume to full
      fully realizing Bach's Dona nobis pacem
You will be swept up to heaven by music's glory
      in this anthem for peace
      as only music, Bach can sing

Sit in the oversized church with swollen audience
      and try not to weep when the alto
      sings Erbarme dich
As she weeps in duo with the violin
      try to hold your tears back
      you cannot

Sit with me, head cocked back, in Cinesphere
      watching the film "Amadeus"
      and don't smile as the ghost of Wolfgang
      torments the aged Salieri

With his incessant laughter while the Romanze
of the D minor piano concerto
winks and nods in the background

Come with me and we'll find our way to the forgotten
church on the outskirts of London
where we can await the powerful
Bone-chilling opening chords of Pärt's Passio
performed by the one-and-only Hilliard Ensemble

Find your way to Nova Scotia and perch yourself on a pew
if there's room amongst the primary school audience
in the white clapboard church
While those Youth-ful Singers from Guelph
sing through their hearts
and empty yours of any misgiving in life

Sit on the edge of my hospital bed
while IV pump clicks and clacks
for I've semi-serendipitously found
the answer to a prayer
Where the oddly placed hands of the gifted old master
play Bach-Busoni's Nun komm transcription
on his apartment Steinway
and I am transported
freed of any medical tether, tenuous bond of mortality

Sing beside me in concert and
Hear my prayer
as Purcell so eloquently pleads
and help me as my praying overwhelms
my ability to sing the line
pray with me, pray for me

Sing beside me in concert and
beware the power, simplicity and urgency
of Sander's Reproaches for Tenebrae

"O my people, what have I done to you,
       how have I offended you?"
No, Lord, You have done nothing
You have not offended
       and we are humbled at the anguish
       inherent to the music
       and you break down at the end of the concert
       oh, do I understand

When Mozart plays the keyboard upside down
       and ridicules other composers
       and poses to fart in the face of the Emperor
And my children laugh to the point of passing
       their own gas
       then I, once again, thank music

In the little churches of Vienna
       over and over two tenors
       sing plainchant
Would you join us, with our little books of notation
       and sing plaintively for the building
       the plastered walls
       the acoustic
       the hunched old lady cleaning in the back corner
       who looks for your donation
       to help keep mortar between the stones

When she plays his Little prelude in E minor
       and loves the music of Bach
       as I sit in the yellow room with two pianos
       with her teacher
Can you close your eyes as I do
       catch the sunlight streaming in
       warming your inner gaze
       and marvel at the sophistication of her playing
       the communication of sheer beauty

I remember standing on the marble ledge
        overseeing the congregation before me
        and singing the upward cascade of
        Allegri's treble
But I remember more, in the pleasantly musty practice room
        singing and singing, especially Christmas carols
        where I knew no bounds
        I could sing with ease and abandonment
        any and every descant line

Could you join the distant memory of
        Toronto Symphony concerts in
        Massey Hall
Filled with children and parents
        and the long-haired percussionist with the eye-patch
        who appeared to be surreptitiously leisure reading
        until the time of his part
        whereupon he never missed a clang or bash
        or beat, bump or thump

I remember seeing Beatlemania
        more than once
        and here they were
My teenaged heart's delight
        it was thrilling
        transforming
        harmonious heart-breaking music
        from humble beginnings to super-stardom and the end
        all too quickly

Across the pond I do recall
        stepping out onto octagonal apron
        gazing out past buttressed nave
        as Ely's lantern-capped cathedral
        stretches beyond my eye
"Rise up, my love, my fair one" we sing
        into a gothic infiniteness

Have you ever sung in an astounding acoustic?
    Come with me, let's try it together
    it's like being wrapped in your warmest, coziest blanket
    and yet underneath you find a consoling emptiness
    spaciousness and depth
No sense that you can and will be enveloped
    and then you sing something, anything
    the sound goes out
    (you can go and get a cup of coffee)
    comes back eventually and surrounds you
    enfolds and bathes you with its
    ambient richness and added lustre
    almost intoxicating
I recommend the Chapel of King's College in Cambridge
    visually stunning and two-dimensional in effect
    four-dimensional in sound

I returned to all of them
    alone
    so contented
    just to be in that space
    Ely and King's and Durham
Durham so palpably ancient with its
    thick Norman pillars, all etched differently
    unbutressed walls
    and I was alone
    with my companions Bede and Cuthbert
    and sat in the quire
    for evensong
    alone but the choir
    perfectly contented

Do you remember that time between adulthood and parenthood
    past teenaged, but not long past
    where you had little responsibility
    little money
    little worry

And you were free, between relationships
    with some time on your young and supple hands
Do you remember that one perfect day
    it is there, I'm certain
    for all of us
    if we don't miss it
    but it is just the one day
And I knew it was coming, having arrived on my own
    at London's Victoria Station from Gatwick
    late and wet and getter wetter
    with bags in tow
    and no idea where I was headed
What to do first
    off to Westminster Cathedral
    for the end of a Latin service
    and to clear my head with incense and smoke
    then down the street to the Abbey
    just because
And there in the pouring rain
    on the front entrance
    simply posted
"Allegri Miserere & Faure Requiem tonight"
    my last concert as a treble
    of course, I go, all loopy-headed with jet lag
    and soaked bags at my feet
    this was two days before Palm Sunday
    and I would fly to Kenya on Easter Monday

Oh, the perfect day, just foreshadowed till now
    such a good day it was, that Good Friday
    up early with cup of tea in my Maze Hill lodging
    train and tube into the city
    back to Westminster Abbey for 11:00
St. John Passion by Victoria in Latin
    austere and direct
    then off to the banking district and St. Paul's for 3:00
    bite of lunch on front steps and feed the birds

Haydn's Seven last words with string quartet
> resonant and haunting
> interspersed with scripture, readings and anthems
> then off back to Westminster
> this time to the Cathedral at 5:30

Plainchant with men only
> black cassocks
> medieval vernacular
> and much smoke
> then to Trafalgar Square
> St. Martin-in-the-Fields for 8:00

And finally Bach's St. John Passion
> treated myself to supper at the
> café in the crypt beforehand
> then completed my perfect day
> with the master's masterwork
> period-performance perfectly placed

How good is Good

Hands-crossing arpeggios he plays
> with joy
> as much as any piece of
> Bach or Mozart or Schumann he knows

Beethoven yet to come though
> perhaps this will change his inclination
> perhaps not
> my quirky in-his-own-world
> musician son

I remember the first Bach that I had to really work through
> the magnificent motet
> Jesu meine Freude
> it seemed such hard toil

Some argue that Handel wrote more sympathetically for the voice
> more naturally, easier
> maybe so
> but Bach understood the human condition far

more deeply
passionately
soulfully
He gave the singer
(almost wrote sinner)
more work in preparation
but in the work, comes the reward
it is never Hallelujah chorus in isolation
light comes through a path connected to darkness
darkness is never avoided
in fact, Bach will always explore darkness
sadness, grief, loss, waywardness
In this, he connects to every human being
and then elevates our sorrow and despair
through music of the most utter beauty
For me, Bach took my labour in preparing this motet
and gave me the gift of "Gute Nacht, o Wesen"
where the tenor sings continuo as a cyclical confession
and I am transported beyond the mere
participation in music
to the ephemeral

I'm sure it was my sixteenth birthday
for I drove myself to the gift of my choosing
my home-away-from home
beloved music shop
And bought a luxurious looking boxed set of Bach
complete orchestral works
carefully set beside me
I left Douglas Street for home
where each record was removed in succession
carefully wiped and de-linted
placed, needle cleaned, aligned and played
Until late that night I lay on the living room floor
as Die Kunst der Fuge finishes
not
and B-A-C-H plays out

this majestic, mysterious final fugue

is left floating away like a balloon

suddenly untethered and instantly disappearing from view

There is no conclusion, denouement

did the master die mid-pen stroke

was he raptured as he inked his name-sake theme

or did he leave his best fugue never to be

concluded

contrapuntal

conundrum

It was a deep pleasure, as you will remember

for me to sing at our wedding

Rosetti's exquisite snow-etched nativity pastiche

in Darke's underlit understated setting

"Enough for him whom cherubim

worship night and day

a breast full of milk

and a manger full of hay"

lovely line to sing, with rolled 'r' in "breast"

and aspirated 'k' at the end of "milk"

as the carol continues to move through the bleak midwinter

the question arises in the final verse

In the end, what can we ever give

one another, other than our very hearts

"Little boy kneels at the foot of the bed,

drooping on little hands, little gold head"

hush, hush, prayer in a song

ushers him on through his days all life-long …

stricken mid-man on the length of the bed

closing his whittled eye, bulgy-lumped head

hush, hush, whisper your prayer

Glenn Douglas Peirson beseeching your care

F

R

A

G

M

E

N

T

S

Chaconne
(notes for a poem)
(April 15, 2007)

> Why does it circle me, this chaconne?
This chaconne, of all chaconnes,
> the one and only chaconne…

It is the soul of music, the very
> essence, no matter when or where I
> hear it … it is the one　.

A singular, crystalline entity of
> what music can be.

of Easter
(March 30, 2008)

warm and unadulterated it enters…

(August 12, 2008)

How like the summer was my absence long
from thee, no pleasure in lengthening year
How helpless I have felt without a song,
with cruel July's heat leaving only fear.

(date unknown)

The body is a fickle thing
        we all know that
but remarkably it works
        so well, harmoniously,
seamlessly, predictably

And of course we take it
        for granted, until it breaksdown
we may complain that without
        a hot shower, swig of
        caffeine, or brisk walk
        we are sub-par for the day

But really,
        really,
                this is not the case
                compared with the daily
                miracle of cellular function
                synaptic connection - our
        continual ticking away

Prose: 2009

Date: January 8, 2009
Subject: health update ...

Happy New Year friends,

Happy Epiphany while we're at it! I know it has been far too long since I have written. I am happy to say that I bring you glad tidings of moderately good joy. The four months following my last communiqué in July were extremely difficult with chemotherapy fall-out. There was a period in the summer when I was in hospital some 25 out of 40 days. Everything was relatively smooth with the treatments in Victoria Hospital in London; it was the week or so afterwards when things would predictably fall apart. After each of the 4 rounds of chemo I developed febrile neutropenia, a well-known but nasty chemo side-effect where one's neutrophils (a major infection-fighting white blood cell) are obliterated and a fever develops. The risks are extremely great when this happens. I was hospitalized the first two times this happened and then with a load of antibiotics and medications was able to (just barely) manage at home after the last 2 rounds of chemo. This extended the length of my treatment period and really wiped me out physically. I've witnessed many patients with neutropenia over the years, but had no idea, no idea, how profoundly awful this condition is ... the only way I could describe it to Mary was a sense of loss of physiological integrity, as if I was breaking down at a molecular level. It was a terribly disturbing state of being. On one occasion I slept for more than 24 hours straight, aside from some brief moments of consciousness. As in the past, it is important to note that these health problems were all treatment-related as opposed to cancer-caused. The only good thing about the consistency of this suffering was its consistency. I always recovered and was able to eat again and regain some measure of strength before the next onslaught. Interestingly I don't really feel traumatized in recalling this now. In fact it all seems somewhat abstract. Pain does not seem to hold much in the way of memory, despite how intense or unrelenting it can be at the time. Early into the treatment period I had a gastric feeding tube implanted which was, just like last year, a wonderfully ambivalent godsend for me.

By early November I was back on track, consuming extraordinary numbers of calories, declining people's altruistically-intentioned offers to donate their extra poundage, and had the G-tube gratefully removed. I have been off work since my treatment began in July and have no realistic return to work date at this point. My strength, my weight, my hemoglobin are all improving. Various side-effects linger from the chemo and will take time. But further treatment is on the near horizon. Mary and I were able to organize the test that I could not get last year, a PET-CT scan, which is a marrying of physiological and anatomical information and gives a window of information in head & neck cancer surveillance that ordinary CT or MRI technology do not. PET-CT can show tumour activity 9 – 12 months before other testing can.

On November 30th we sauntered down to Buffalo, were searched by federal agents at the border just for fun, and I had the PET-CT scan the next morning. As expected, I was not found to be cancer free, but my sinus appeared to show a negligible amount of tumour and the mediastinal nodes (space between the lungs) have regressed. This puts me into candidacy for further radiation treatment, likely a focal approach, which is much lower in side-effects from what I had last year. What needs to be determined is what specific type of treatment and where will this happen. The chances are reasonably high that I could end up back in the States, as Canada lags behind in the newest radiation techniques. This will involve some major hoop jumping as we would need OHIP to cover me for out-of-country treatment (or we could sell everything we own, perhaps our children too, rob a few banks and that should cover it [*please note the hyperbole*]).

I have continued on a very new medication, a so-called biological agent, called panitumumab since finishing chemo. I might be the only head & neck patient in this country on the medication outside of research trials. I've had seven infusions of P-mab, about every 3 weeks, not covered by OHIP unfortunately, and forming a good long-term treatment plan until I developed an allergy to the medication after my last dose. Now this needs to be reevaluated as well. Later this week I will receive my 8th treatment with the P-mab after a number of days of "pre-medication" to hopefully reduce allergic symptoms. I will also see an allergist that my oncologist recommends to seek further wisdom.

The bottom line? Advocating for optimal treatment, creative thinking around our options, and keeping vigilant and forward moving is basically a full-time job for Mary and me. And thank God for her ... Mary is tenacious around moving forward with my treatment, pragmatic in the running of our lives, and provides a foundation of love and care for me and Theo and Henry. Alright, she is a tad crabby in the mornings and can lack the precision of logic in certain decision-making (and of course appreciates when I point this out). Last July she beautifully organized the acquisition and transportation of a "soft-tub" (portable hot tub) for our cottage … for a perfect little spot under the cedars behind the cottage and looking out over Lake Huron. The only problem was that the tub didn't hold water … actually this turned out to be a rather critical problem. To make a long story short, eventually the tub was returned to the vendor for repair, whereupon he quickly changed his tune from one of blaming Mary for the problem to one of contrition. He had installed the liner incorrectly. It is now fixed, runs like a Porsche, and sits on our back patio for the winter (before another migration north to the cottage). On December 28th we hosted our 16th sibs breakfast, an almost full-day sit-down multiple course breakfast for 13 of our sibs and their spouses, and finished up the afternoon with shifts of hot-tubbing complete with flutes of Prosecco. We've evolved from tobogganing after our party to skating and then long walks on green Christmases and now to post-prandial digestion in the spa. I did muse that next year Mary and I might need to hire staff to feed our sibs, so as not to slow the progression of collective sloth.

The Christmas holidays have been, as always, a special time for us as a family and also with our extended families. Would that everyone was as blessed as we are with the true affection and good spirit of our families. Mary and I have spent some memorable time with our kids by the fire watching some lovely old movies and just simply enjoying each others' company. We have for many years kept the Twelve Days of Christmas, with this year no exception. We hold back many little gifts and godparent presents and dole them out over the Christmas season. This finished yesterday with Epiphany where we watched the unsung and evocative film called The Nativity, devoured Mary's braised beef dish, and the kids opened their final gift, a little gem of a rosewood box in which lay resins of frankincense and myrrh (we skipped the gold). Perfect for incense on the fire.

Perhaps I make our Christmas and family life sound idyllic, and though it is singular, and reflection always adds luster, there is a current of anxiety that flows underneath our daily existence. Christmas and many other family activities lend healthy distraction, but we do worry and the work of getting adequate and optimal health care is exhausting. But, this is our reality and we are accustomed to it and plow on (such a Canadian metaphor).

Henry is just starting basketball, loves his myriad of Christmas gifts, except perhaps his "pooh-pooh doll" which I bought for him after a month of incessant teasing from me that he wanted one and forgot to ask Santa, and continues with his music and varied interests. Theo is singing with her Guelph Youth Singers choir III for a professional recording this week and then preparing to head on tour to Nova Scotia at the end of April. She is playing jazz, a Beethoven sonata, her commissioned pieces from our friend Barrie Cabena, and a Haydn concerto in her piano repertoire these days. She had a marvellous experience accompanying an orchestra of 150 in Largo from Vivaldi's Winter in November in Toronto. She continues to swim regularly, loves her school activities and responsibilities, and has taken to babysitting with a passion. Mary is back to work after the holidays and continues to almost single-handedly support teenage gynecological health in our vicinity (I'm so proud!). Me, I am busy with the life and work of our church, supporting my practice as best possible, pursuing music at every opportunity, and generally enjoying life's little moments (which is where life lives, by the way).

You, our friends, have continued to offer us immeasurable support and love … whether embodied by good wishes, messages, cards, or little gifts, a book, music, a jar of Marmite, flowers, or food silently left at the back door, or those silent prayers that we don't know about but sense, or gestures for our children, who continue to seem incredibly normal in the face of our abnormal life together.

Glenn

Here is Tennyson's classic new year's poem, which to my ears is startlingly modern through and through (I was thinking of excerpting it, but couldn't):
Ring out, wild bells, to the wild sky,
The flying cloud, the frosty light:
The year is dying in the night;
Ring out, wild bells, and let him die.

Ring out the old, ring in the new,
Ring, happy bells, across the snow:
The year is going, let him go;
Ring out the false, ring in the true.

Ring out the grief that saps the mind,

For those that here we see no more,
Ring out the feud of rich and poor,
Ring in redress to all mankind.

Ring out a slowly dying cause,
And ancient forms of party strife;
Ring in the nobler modes of life,
With sweeter manners, purer laws.

Ring out the want, the care, the sin,
The faithless coldness of the times;
Ring out, ring out my mournful rhymes,
But ring the fuller minstrel in.

Ring out false pride in place and blood,
The civic slander and the spite;
Ring in the love of truth and right,
Ring in the common love of good.

Ring out old shapes of foul disease,
Ring out the narrowing lust of gold;
Ring out the thousand wars of old,
Ring in the thousand years of peace.
Ring in the valiant man and free,
The larger heart, the kindlier hand;
Ring out the darkness of the land,
Ring in the Christ that is to be.

Alfred, Lord Tennyson (written about 1850)

Dear family,

Just wanted to keep you all in the loop. As most of you may be aware, this is a particularly busy week for us and thank goodness Mary's off most of the week because of exams. We found out on Friday that I was to have a consultation today at the Gamma Knife Centre at Toronto Western. We had been waiting for this since seeing my radiation oncologist in London in early December. Tomorrow we head to London for a consult with an allergist/immunologist regarding my reaction to P-mab (which went much better early this month with a nice cocktail of anti-allergy drugs). And Friday I am in Cambridge for review with the oncologist there and likely my P-mab infusion.

We also received the great news from Dr. Chouinard in Cambridge that the pharmaceutical company (Amgen) will assist with the cost of the P-mab. We don't have details as to how much assistance this will be nor when it will start. I first contacted Amgen to apply for their financial assistance program last July when in hospital with my first round of chemo! Ah, good things come to those who wait, or so it has been said.

With regard to today, the most exciting aspect was the driving ... not particularly fun, but no harm incurred, even though a snow plow turned left into a highway U-turn access from the right-most lane and immediately in front of us! Dr. M. met with us along with her neurosurgical colleague and was clearly well-prepared after studying my imaging. I had sent her a personal letter about my story and need for her assessment last week along with the most recent CT scan. She wanted my medical story in a nutshell (which we have down to an art form).

The bottom line is this and it is somewhat technical: gamma knife, the focal radiation technique that Dr. M. uses, is very, very specific and the residual tumour in my sinus is not clearly demarcated enough to use this method. She sees two other radiation techniques as very feasible and very hopeful: tomo therapy, which is available in Canada and would likely be administered in London, which is relatively focal but requires multiple treatments, probably 6-weeks of M-F; and cyber knife, not in Canada, more specific than tomo and requires a small number of treatments but is also smaller in its field of treatment. She feels that tomo is probably the best option for me. She thinks that some form of field radiation or tomo is likely appropriate for my chest and can be done at the same time.

Dr. M. is organizing two next steps: an MRI in Toronto and a consult with another radiation oncologist at Princess Margaret who is an expert in cyber knife and actually determines if Ontario patients qualify for out-of-country funding. These should both happen in the next week or two.

We are also awaiting an opinion from Pittsburgh.

Summary? I definitely need some form of radiation sooner than later (not new news, but now with further support) and the options are being narrowed and we know who all the players are.

We would appreciate you not sharing this particular information with others. It is too strange and technical and indeterminate at present. We are comfortable with where we're at and I, for one, am very happy to be past today's appointment. But we don't need to be answering the many questions that could come our way from other people about these details.

Thanks, as always, for your support and love.

Glenn & Mary

Dear family,

Here is the current lay of the land. A week ago Friday I spoke with Dr. S. at Princess Margaret Hospital. We had met him the week previous and were impressed with his knowledge and forward thinking. He had spoken of a limited number of stereotactic radiation treatments. However, in following up with him, after he had conferred at MD Anderson in Texas with colleagues, he recommended tomo therapy, which is a more specific form of radiation (using 360 degree treatment approach and daily CT scanning to make adjustments) and more specific in treating tumour, but still requires many treatment sessions.

So last Wednesday I was evaluated for radiation planning back in London. Sara joined Mary and me. I'm sure you all know that her knowledge and support have been invaluable to us. I am looking at possibly 6 weeks of radiation to the sinus ... hopefully less treatments if possible and appropriate. We won't find out the exact schedule until my first day, which is Feb. 23. I remember finishing radiation in July 07 and feeling thankful that I would never have to see the treatment mask again. Well, they made me a new one on Wednesday.

The upside? A certain reassurance of treatment, being in the plan, so to speak. No more agitating as to what to do and who to do it. My face has started swelling again just this week, and it will be consoling to get the treatment under way.

The downside? Fear of side-effects, the daily grind of driving, a certain closure of life for us ... hopefully this time will not be so devastating and we can maintain a sense of normalcy. But, we prepare for a more difficult path.

What next? My chest will be assessed after the sinus is done. Likely radiation for the chest and likely many weeks of that, but possibly in Kitchener. In the future, perhaps even more chemo!?! We will not think too far ahead. We knew this was coming, but we had honestly thought it would be a shorter course of treatment.

We had toyed with another sun-filled holiday this winter. Not to be. So we muse on a chance of taking the kids to Quebec City in the Spring, and dream of travelling with them to England next Fall. They continue to be well and vibrant despite their somewhat stressed parents of late. Theo is off to a dance tonight (!!). I'm hoping she'll hate the music and craziness ... but that's just a father's protective instincts. Henry's school is looking into some enrichment for him. He wrote this name-acronym in library class last week (honestly, at 8, it's not egocentric, aside from the normal egocentrism):

> Handsome
> Extremely handsome
> No more handsomes!!!!!
> Really, really handsome
> Yes, I will stop handsomes

OK, the man has his own particular brain. Entertaining indeed.

That's it for now, except to say that our life may get more difficult over the next 2 or 3 months. My major concern is ensuring Mary's sanity, especially if I am not able to be helpful in the day-to-day routines. She will continue, more or less, her usual work schedule through this time.

As always, thank you for your love, care and support.

Love,
Glenn (& Mary)

Well, dear friends,

Time for another update. I have my laptop sitting on my lap (hey, they could market that!) in the chemo clinic at Cambridge Hospital. No chemo, remember, but I continue to receive this cutting-edge drug Panitumumab every 3 weeks by infusion. The good news here is that I've just received coverage for the drug from the pharmaceutical company. We've been trying every angle for financial assistance for the P-mab since last July, and it's finally paid-off, so to speak. My allergy consult resulted in a protocol for the P-mab which has so far prevented the reactions I spoke of in my last email.

As I mentioned in January, my plethora of recent imaging has shown that I continue <u>not</u> to be cancer free. To be honest, I have never been free of cancer, in true remission, since my treatment began almost 2 years ago. The disease dose appear more localized, hence the planning for further radiation after last summer-fall's chemotherapy. To make a long-ish story short, today was my first dose of re-radiation to my sinus, a technique called tomotherapy, in London. (Yes, then back to Cambridge for the P-mab ... a full hospital tour day ... the bus filled with all my blue-haired compatriots is also stopping at a casino and knick-knack emporium.) We did investigate all the radiation options, including various stereotactic hypo-fractionated approaches (go ahead, do some "Googling"!), and this technique appears to be the correct one for my case.

The good news from today? Instead of a possible 6 weeks, they've scheduled me for 15 treatments, which is 3 weeks of driving to London Monday through Fridays. This minimizes the "grind" factor. In 2007 we accumulated 12,000 km of London driving. We don't need to become any more familiar with the route than is absolutely necessary.

This still leaves treatment of my chest as the next question. Hopefully this will happen not long after the sinus re-treatment and might be possible in Kitchener, which is much closer to home. Basically, we are looking at another 3 month chunk of life devoted to treatment. The past month or so has been highly stressful, always the case when leading up to the next treatment step. There is a strange comfort to being back in treatment, having something done when you are certain it's needed. Just in the past two weeks the right side of my face has started swelling again, very disturbing for me and Mary. So, let's crank it up again.

Don't get me wrong. Ramping up one's emotions, strengthening one's body, re-girding one's loins is no fun or easy or simple process. There is a chronic and diminishing fatigue to not escaping the need for treatment. However, this is my lot, for whatever reason, our lot in life at present. We pray for chronicity of disease and we've had that for 2 years now. We neither put our heads in the sand nor dwell in despair.

The truth is that my chances of cure are small, but my chance of living well and longer are good. This is our reality. Mary and I are optimists by choice and necessity, though some days don't jive with this positively-minded model. We have always been excellent communicators with one another, even when she is wrong (oops … I am now receiving some clearly-communicated feedback here), but there is an undercurrent of anxiety that we share. It oscillates underneath our life, occasionally splashing through and dampening our spirits, but even as we cope well, have fun with our kids, and live life, the undercurrent is there, often unspoken of, coursing along, unwanted but recognized.

So that is us at present. Reconnected to the structure of treatment, a vital blend of down and up-side. My focus? Aside from Theo and Henry, always wonderfully grounding, I look forward to the April 4th Tactus concert. We've commissioned our dear friend Barrie Cabena to create a choral work for this concert: "The many masks of Mad Matthew, the mummer", maybe might manifest a multitude of meandering meanings (sorry), but is actually a stunning mini-oratorio for choir, organ, and narrator. It is a deep pleasure for me that my dad will be narrator for this, along with our great friend Michael Bloss on organ. Aside from Barrie's work, we will be exploring our usual treasure trove of Lenten masterworks, including Bach, Purcell, Mozart, Tallis and Byrd, as well as the Oscar-winning song from Slumdog Millionaire (as Borat would say, "… not!"). Actually, Peter Gabriel's "Down to Earth" is a much better song. Actually, **WALL**·E is a much better movie.

I look forward to scurrying off to Niagara this weekend for our annual Peirson family scurry-off-to-Niagara-weekend. I look forward to travelling to Nova Scotia with Theo and Lukas (my nephew) with Guelph Youth Singers in April. I look forward to Theo and Henry performing at Kiwanis just before that. Perhaps most of all, I look forward to a break from treatment and perhaps a summer where I can truly spend some restorative time at our cottage!

Glenn

It seems that his very soul
was formed
by the sparse and shapely chant,
and the austere polyphonic weavings
of mass and motet,
which he sang with innocent and infectious joy.

> (from *The many masks of Mad Matthew, the mummer ...*
> tacit permission from Barrie Cabena)

Date: April 5, 2009
Subject: Mad Matthew, etc.

Dear Friends,

First off, dear Barrie, you have been incredibly appreciative of our performance of your marvellous work. Let's just be clear that the honour was ours. More specifically, I feel quite privileged that you offered this perfect possibility to me in response to my long, slow inquiry about a commission.

Secondly, Michael, Dad, your contributions were absolutely excellent last night. In particular, I would say that *Mad Matthew* sounded incredibly comfortable, natural under your fingers, Michael. And Ralph, your narration was exactly the style and approach that the work deserved and needed.

Finally, dear Tactus, what a remarkably argued and executed concert. As you know, this program was dear to my heart, still is. I am so gratified with how the whole thing spun out, especially with *Mad Matthew* as the focal point. I found the experiment with our different singing positions very successful, very intimate (hush, Kirk). The flow of the program, from piece to piece, was equally gratifying.

I, however, struggled with my physical self last night, and in hindsight, not surprisingly. Thankfully Marcus was on his game, and hadn't had any hockey pucks ricochet off his larynx recently. Rehearsing for this concert has been wonderfully therapeutic for me over these past weeks. But it has been a distinct struggle in terms of how I've been feeling. Rehearsing is one thing, performing another. I rather hit the wall last night and struggled to control my breathing, especially in quiet passages, and control my pulse, create the comfort zone that makes the concert experience so special. Well, I coped (I'm good at that) and thanks to a bit of corporal punishment at the interval (Sara-Lynn in her dominatrix role), settled further in the second half.

It didn't help that most of my loved ones were in attendance and fully visible through the entire concert (damn the SJK lighting system). So I performed a few mental gymnastics, pondered basketball mid-Purcell, considered new door knobs for our front hall during Bach, and anticipated my left-over summer sausage sandwich (a little alliteration for Dr. Cabena there) during Tallis' Ordinal. But mental tricks have only so much power compared with music's ability to cut through just about any kind of blockade. Comfortably into my sandwich image, text distraction, and only needing to survive 40 seconds, depending on Catherine's final fermata, of this exquisite Tallis, it hit me that I used this tune and text over and over again while bolted under my mask during radiation.

And the one day that I didn't have Tallis' Ordinal as my mantra? Barrie's opening chorus "Many Masks" took over, out-of-the-blue, so it seemed. And yet here was this most gifted composer's new work, all about our masks and Matthew's extraordinarily symbiotic relationship with his, juxtaposed against me living the masked life, literally and daily, in a most ambivalent experience. I hate the mask, and yet have learned to use this time for clear and focused meditation. I love the mask for its potentially life-giving properties, but can't wait to get away from it. And then I hear with my inner ear: "Many masks, so many masks to hide our faces ..."

My life is such that I do not know what my long-term prospects are for Tactus let alone for many other tender matters. Thank you all for making *Mad Matthew* such a memorable, stand-out concert.

Love,
Glenn

Dear family,

As you know, we are at another juncture of treatment starting this week. That is not particularly what I am writing about. Really, I am purely venting ... self-therapy for my irritation of the week. Sara was with Mary and me yesterday, so she knows of what I am about to speak.

In all of our driving to London over these past three years, somewhere around 20,000 km under all sorts of traffic, weather and construction circumstances, we had not received one speeding ticket ... until yesterday. I will attempt to use as little French as possible in this message, but I am simple writing you to get it out, as I am still pissed off at Officer "Chip-on-her-shoulder-I-am-not-a-softy-look-at-my-testicles-you-think-you-can-pass-me".

The three of us were driving home from London after my fourth radiation treatment of the week, after meeting with the oncologist and going over the treatment plan in detail. As we were crossing Woodstock in a 100 km/hr zone, I carefully passed Officer should-have-had-testicles at about 115, when she was about 112. I then signalled and pulled back into the same lane. Shortly thereafter the speed limit reduced to 80 in a construction zone. I reduced to 102 and put on my cruise control and was then passed by numerous vehicles without passing another myself. She (I use the term loosely) was still behind me ... as I was completely aware.

We drove along another 10 minutes perhaps, chatting away about this and that. And then, shit, on went her blue & red & white lights. I knew I was in trouble right away. Did I know what the speed limit was? Yes, I did, but I was travelling under the traffic speed. Still speeding sir. I slowed into the construction zone. Not soon enough and only down to 96 at one point.

Ma'am, Officer, can I tell you what our story is? (Reader's Digest version, tons of travel, safe driving, no tickets, radiation today, etc.) Everyone's got a story sir

... if I didn't give out tickets because of stories, I wouldn't give out tickets at all ... besides construction workers are being killed by speeders.

Really?? (I mean I read the paper daily, and I haven't heard one story in these past years of workers being killed by speeders)

Officer-your-my-first-example-of-the-day comes back after a long delay and tells me what a favour she has done for me. She hasn't indicated that construction workers were present on my offense, otherwise I would have had a mandatory court appearance. And just how would I be able to do that in my present condition, Officer?

So she ticketed me for 103 in an 80 construction zone, $110 (no big deal) and 3 demerit points (irritating). Meanwhile, "rate-limited" trucks were bombing by and after departing, I drove 110 through the zone and was constantly passed.

What bugs me? I drive well and safely and for me, this was slow driving! Apparently my travel story to London is the same as almost anyone else on the 401 (really, honestly Officer?). And construction workers are dying by the dozens because of criminals like me.

I just didn't need her $&*#!!

I explained, just before we left, that I have worked professionally with the police for many years and have respect for their duties. I understand the responsibility of her job, but was disappointed in her as a human being. Hey, I didn't even swear at her.

Thanks for listening, now I feel better ... maybe,

Glenn

PS. today most vehicles were travelling 120 through the construction zone!

May 30, 2009

Dear Family,

Mary and I thought we should just make sure you're all up-to-date with my current treatment goings-on. We know you are all generally aware of what's happening presently, but there are a few details worth being clear on.

Thankfully I am now 19 treatments finished of 25 for this chest radiation. So I finish up on Monday June 8th (not that we're counting the seconds). It will be weeks of recovery afterwards, but I will not be travelling to London every day, which is enough of a reward in itself. The past few weeks have been very stressful for us, as I have become increasingly symptomatic from the treatment, end-of-year wrap-up life has been busy, and Mary's work is in its busiest stretch of the year (all those pre-summer PAP smears and birth control prescriptions!). The strain on Mary as I withdraw from being a helpful husband and father is tough and we've had to do this all too long now. The illness fatigue is in itself fatiguing.

This bout of radiation has proven much tougher than the sinus re-radiation back in February-March. Part of the difficulty is that here I am in treatment again, yet not fully recovered from the sinus radiation. This is also a relatively large field of radiation at present. I also developed a sinus infection about 2 weeks ago and am on antibiotics.

So we are coping, thanks to all of you and some wonderful support from our church. Dublin has volunteered to provide us with lunches three days a week (when Mary is working) and a number of dinners as well ... that's real pastoral care as far as we're concerned!

I have been struggling with some specific back pain over the past couple of months, and had wondered if any news would arise from testing at the time of my radiation planning late in March. Heard nothing from those various tests, but still worried about the pain.

I started radiation for my chest the day after returning from Nova Scotia with Theo and Lukas, and discovered that my radiation plan was completely changed from what was originally discussed. Nonetheless, we were pleased with the new tomotherapy plan, which doesn't require "gaited" treatment for respiratory movement. The therapists said they would speak with my oncologist and he met with me just outside the treatment room on day #2.

We like Dr. Y., his approach and direct manner, very much. He spent about 20 minutes with me at the computer, and did highlight that there is a metastasis in 10th thoracic vertebra. They had already factored this into the treatment plan and, in fact, had already treated me the day before without my knowledge! Will wonders never cease at LRCC?

So the bad news is that I have a single spinal bone spot of cancer. The good news is that it is treatable and he maintains that the plan continues to be one of aggressive, curative intent. To be honest, this unwanted news is not really any worse than the chest mets diagnosed last June. We have decided to only let family know these details ... too difficult to help people understand such particular and tricky information. We do not want to have to manage people's pity or encounter any undue pessimism. You all know that my prognosis is uncertain, but we continue living optimistically and with hope, despite my current cruddy symptoms. My face has become quite strange around my affected eye and this seems to be post-radiation effect, but I very well may need this to be looked into as well.

Our oncology team is pursuing another PET scan for about 4 weeks after this treatment ... hopefully not too many political hoops! We did, believe it or not, actually get reimbursed by OHIP about 2 weeks ago for the PET from Dec. 1 in Buffalo. If this radiation plan and then follow-up testing goes well, we may get a real break from treatment for a stretch ... what a lovely thought.

That is our nutshell right now. I'm getting there. Mary's schedule will quieten soon. The kids' extracurriculars are finishing up. And we are contemplating matters cottage!

Love,
Glenn

Date: May 31, 2009
Subject: health update

Hello again, dear friends,

I tend to communicate with you through this imperfect medium at a specific juncture, usually the start of some phase of treatment or with something newsworthy. Presently I am a month into chest radiation in London and am a month behind in keeping you up-to-date.

I know many of you would tell me not to worry about being slow in getting more information to you, but I honestly do this as much for us as for you. It is helpful for Mary and me to know that you know what is going on – a focus for your care, concern, prayer. There is also something therapeutic to putting words down (pen to paper?!?) and getting outside of the all-encompassing world of cancer treatment. As much as we do not define our lives by cancer, there is an element of surrender to the rigor, side-effects and in-your-face nature of treatment. We do very much look forward to hopefully a relatively treatment-free summer … ah, we are easy to please.

I also know that for some of you, seeing the byline "health update" is anxiety provoking, as in "what bomb will I drop in this email?" Well, I have no particular bombs to drop today. Nor do I have any particular good news. Just news.

Radiation started hot on the heels of returning from travel with my daughter Theo and nephew Lukas on Guelph Youth Singers' (GYS) tour to Nova Scotia. More on this wonderful experience later. But freshly back with trip fatigue and lobster lingering in my gullet, I steam-rolled into my treatment plan on May 4th. I arrived in London that morning to find that my radiation plan was completely changed from what had been anticipated, but with good reason. All the fancy planning showed that I do not need the radiation "gaited" to my respirations, as my chest movement is minimal and will not interfere with the radiation targeting. This allows the oncologist and his team to use a potentially better technique for me. Very good, but in the 6 weeks since planning they could have let me know, phoned, emailed, sent up a smoke signal. But this is London and on-par for the utter lack of civil communication within the massive cancer centre bureaucracy.

We are extremely good at letting go of these irritations, even if fundamental. I haven't been as good at letting go of the speeding ticket I received later that week (102 in an 80 zone on the 401 while travelling slower than traffic speed). She was one officious officer and despite our story, almost 20,000 km of travel to London in the past three years and my pathetic chemo-tinged driver's license photo, there was no sympathy in the reflection of her mirrored machismo sunglasses. Lessons in humility know no bounds.

So I am now 19 treatments into a 25 treatment schedule. My British friends will be amused that I finish on a Monday to make up for the hospital closure on our national holiday celebrating Victoria's birthday (honestly!). Luckily I should be out of the treatment loop before the annual celebration of HRH's corgis.

We are coping and celebrating the caring nature of our family and especially our church family, which has almost single-handedly taken on the task of feeding us on radiation days (and doing so very well!). This is Mary's busiest work season of the year … all those pre-summer public (pubic?) health interventions with high school students. Theo and Henry are in the midst of end-of-year wrap-up which, thankfully, is wrapping up. Theo heads to university for the next three days, part of the grade 6 graduation program, and we certainly expect her to come home with an honours with distinction degree. She was recently awarded a Kiwanis scholarship for her piano performance in the Festival. Henry and Theo had the honour of accepting Kiwanis awards on behalf of GYS as well.

I mentioned that I would come back to the Nova Scotian tour, where as part of my chaperone role I offered to send a daily journal back to choristers' parents. The week in Truro was a singular experience and, in the end, despite many fascinating activities, experiences, tours of Tatamagouche and Halifax, the music won out, as it should, as highlight of the week. Not just in the superb concerts, from little quintessential Maritime clapboard church to Halifax cathedral, but virtually all the time – almost incessant, mesmerizing, beautiful singing, on the bus, in line for ice cream, individually, in little groups, in appreciation for all the wonderful hospitality.

As we all know, life can seem exceedingly complex, but at times it is not. In fact, happiness, contentment, meaningfulness are not complicated. Hanging out with 26 young people who are cultivating their art, expressing so easily and openly their love of music, and just having a wonderful time together … this is simple and clear, and I was privileged to be riding on their coattails.

Love,
Glenn

When I sat Thursday night directly behind the choir in Fall River, I had some time to ponder what these young people are doing. Or at least what they are doing musically. I don't know that they really appreciate the scope of their endeavour. I am passionate about music, especially choral music. I have performed much, attended many superb concerts, and listen to vocal music of the highest order. I don't believe that I have encountered any ensemble that communicates any better than this group of GYSers. Really. Music is, in the end, communication. The message may be complex and nuanced; it may require training and discipline; it may speak at a level beyond the simple analysis of its expression. These young choristers are part of something quite special, heightened by the tour experience, and certainly a sum more than its parts. This, perhaps, the kids don't quite yet understand. Their collective communication is profound and beautifully open. It is communication beyond its purpose.
And it has made this week an absolute joy to behold.
(from Day 5 SEVEC GYS tour)

June 17, 2009

Dear family,

As most of you are aware we have been awaiting important information on the status on my newer facial swelling and eye problems. This started to arise around the Victoria Day weekend, when we wondered if I had developed a sinus infection (which I indeed may have). But the symptoms didn't fully abate and two weeks ago I asked my chest oncologist to send me to the ophthalmology clinic.

I was seen by Dr. A., who consulted post-initial radiation in Aug. 2007, and he suggested that the suspicious areas be biopsied. I saw him again the next day (June 5th) and underwent the rather unpleasant chore of being awake while he dug around in my upper eyelid with local freezing. He also sampled on area on my temple. Then the following Monday, my head & neck oncologist, the infamous Dr. H., did a needle biopsy of a swollen lymph node at the angle of my jaw. He had also ordered an urgent MRI a few days previously.

So we have been waiting on the biopsy results and also waiting for a booking for this "urgent" MRI.

This is a strange circumstance, as you will recall my sinus was re-radiated in March and now these symptoms have cropped up very suddenly in the past few weeks. All the specialists feel that the swelling and lumps are cancerous. We are prepared for this, not welcoming of it, but my news does seem to always be bad. When we worry about a new symptom or sign, it always turns out to be what we most feared.

So after a couple of calls to London last week, we finally heard about my MRI, which is scheduled for this Sunday morning (Happy Fathers' Day!). And then late yesterday afternoon, after being told the biopsy results would probably be available last Friday, I heard from Dr. H. that the needle biopsy is positive for cancer (same type as my sinus tumour).

This is indeed shitty news.

We have yet to hear about the biopsies Dr. A. performed and the MRI will give more understanding to the anatomy of what is happening. This new disease must be all outside the field of sinus radiation from this past winter. There was no evidence of any of this on the PET scan in Dec. nor in CT of my head in Feb. from just before the radiation started.

What does this mean? Hard to say at present. We will meet next week with Dr. W., my chemo specialist, and I know he has some tricks up his sleeve. Dr. H. already has a preliminary radiation plan. We may need to seek the advice of a radiation oncologist we saw at Princess Margaret in Jan. We may need to look at some techniques not available in Canada. Even some focal surgery is a possibility.

Our objective is for me to live for a decent while yet! My second objective is to get back some sense of normalcy to the right side of my face.

Please understand, the tall hooded fellow with the black robe and boney fingers and long sickle isn't hanging around me. He might be in the other room, but I'd just as soon find him and throw him out of the house head first. He has no place in our lives at present! If not for these facial woes, I would be very pleased with my current state. My breathing clear, my voice strong, my strength stronger, my back pain-free, my appetite relatively free-range ... all good signs after the chest radiation. Back to our mantra, "one day at a time".

We are hanging in there, with a steady flow of prayer, an undercurrent of anxiety, a worry for the possible loss of another summer's promise, and the need to carry on with life as we know it.

We will keep you posted as a plan comes into place.

Love,
Glenn

Dear family,

We were in London yesterday ostensibly for chemo #2, but given my myriad of unpleasant side-effects in the past couple of weeks, the treatment was predictably deferred for a week. The good news in this? First, we can sneak up to the cottage for 5 days (as originally planned before our summer planning derailed) and my symptoms are quelling and should be at bay when I hit chemo (or it hits me) again next Thursday.

When we were up north the week after school ended and about 5 days after chemo #1, I developed the dreaded fever. This indicated that I had neutropenia, which is the state of critically low infection-fighting white cells. I had this quite badly after each round of chemo last summer and usually landed in hospital in Guelph. Well, we pulled out our old bag of tricks, found some good quality antibiotics in our cupboard and monitored things overnight. Luckily the temperature settled, but mucositis attacked my mouth and I was in some serious pain with eating/drinking problems. Nothing our friendly neighbourhood Lion's Head doctor friends couldn't help ... morphine to the rescue. We managed the week and got just enough nutrition into me.

I checked in with my local oncologist in Cambridge the following Monday and my bloodwork was decent. But within the next few days I developed strange rashes all over the place. The worst of which was a burn-like lesion just below my left shoulder blade. I also developed nasty painful ulcers on the outside of my mouth on my lower face and a few other patches scattered here and there. No fun.

Again we used our old bag of tricks to keep things at bay. The important matter, though, is that all of the tumour deposits around my eye showed dramatic shrinkage, some to the point of disappearing to touch. My eye is still terribly swollen and I wear a patch much of the time, partly just to avert the inevitable staring that comes with displaying my face in public.

We made it again to the cottage this past weekend, when up to the last minute I really didn't think I could muster the energy. But thank goodness ... Henry's starring role as the English King (with the appropriate accent) in his operetta Friday evening and then a wonderful weekend celebrating Theo's 12th with two of her friends. This after she had the early week at Gramma and Grampa's for some dress-making, cooking, divine domesticity (yes, Jim is talented at all these things) and a birthday celebration at Westmount. She had a very good week!

So the plan is to carry on with this same chemo, but reduce the dose of the 2nd agent, likely the cause of the major side-effects. It turns out the burn-like rash is indeed a burn. It exactly corresponds to an area in my chest radiation plan from May that exited my left upper back. I had no skin symptoms at the time of treatment, but the chemo has now caused a classic "radiation recall" reaction. The oncology team was so impressed with the reaction and how it mapped out that before we knew it, I had a resident in snooping at me and the Health Sciences' professional photographer to document the lesion ... how exciting.

We have a better plan for treating all of this, hopefully avoiding most of the unpleasantries in the future; and today I feel much perkier, much less pain.

Last note to you I mentioned that we are "back in the trench with helmets on, weapons at the ready and aid station nearby". Well, I couldn't have been more right about this trench-warfare allusion. And so we continue, one day at a time, measuring the unencumbered moments generously! Now if we can just time my treatments well so we can be out of the trench on August 22nd ... this is a good goal!!

Love,
Glenn

July 20, 2009

Happy summer to you, friends,

For those of you not of Southern Ontario persuasion, it has been unseasonably cool and fairly damp, when we usually grapple with oppressive humidity and arid gardens by mid-summer. Sadly this made for a less-than-delicious strawberry season, as berries were under-ripe and dilute of sweetness. However, we could certainly host a British Open golf tournament ... yesterday perhaps hit a high of 17C with cool winds off the lake, making for woodstove and sweater weather on the Bruce Peninsula.

We are enjoying a five day respite at our sanctuary here, despite the difficulty in hauling my bones on any journey these days. Much has happened since my last missive at the end of May. I sit here with the computer warming my lap while Dad chances a swim with Henry (I think they are covertly geared towards the hot tub if truth be told) and Mum has treated Mary and Theo to lunch in Wiarton as a break in routine. It is warmer today and the dappled sun off the lake is lustrous and warming to the eye. I sit listening to some Stokowski transcriptions of Bach, lush and full-bodied and nothing that Bach would have ever imagined, at least in his day. The old genius probably stoops on his perch now and smiles at the remarkably emotive and romantic settings of his music such as these. Expansive and still translucent music perfect for the expansive limestone-shored setting of this great ocean-lake and conducive to a reflective mindset for letter writing.

We have had a most difficult past 6 weeks, since just after I last wrote. I was close to finishing my chest radiation plan when I noticed some lumps around my eye and a swollen gland at the angle of my jaw. Strange and perplexing, given that I had completed re-radiation to my sinus just in March. My less-than-favoured oncologist wanted to treat a possible sinus infection and watch things. Within short order it was clear that this was not improving. I was seen urgently at the ophthalmology clinic, where a couple of these lesions were biopsied (less-than-fun). The various specialists involved at that point all felt the changes were cancerous. This was remarkably disappointing and discombobulating for us.

Sure enough the biopsies came back positive for my particular sinus cancer. All the radiation oncologist could surmise was that the cancerous nodules had arisen from cells just outside the field of sinus re-treatment from the winter. We reconnected with our beloved medical oncologist. He advised more chemo and likely superficial radiation after tumour shrinkage.

So I sit here now, right eye patched and swollen shut by inflammation, face marred by ugly hemorraghic patches due to chemo rash, and my left upper back carefully dressed for a burn wound from a "radiation recall" reaction where the chemo has elicited a "remembered" radiation response in an area that affected the skin originally. Yes, I am a bit of a mess ... likely anemic, having fought off a fever and critical drop in white cells two weeks ago, and continuing to battle mucositis, which is the chemo-caused deterioration of my mouth membranes (I strive to avoid a feeding tube this summer!). Now, don't get my wrong, I am not endeavouring to give you a list of my complaints, nor I am particularly candy-coating my all too familiar current experience. This simply is the reality of chemo and radiation side-effects for head & neck cancer, at least for my specific journey. Generally we are carrying on, day-at-a-time per usual, and preparing ourselves for the next treatment. Chemo #2 should be this Thursday in London, after deferral last week because of the side-effects.

We will attempt to get up here as much as possible. Theo and Henry finished their respective weeks of operetta camp on the past two Friday evenings. They were wonderful in each of their closing performances, Henry as the self-taught-accented actor/musician English King in The Gypsy's Reward and Theo as the multi-talented pianist/singer/actor/script-writer in The Phantom of the Music Room. They each have overnight camps upcoming and then Suzuki piano institute in August at Laurier University (which I greatly look forward to!). We have Mary's brother Paul and lovely-wife-to-be Sarah's wedding later in August, where Theo will be a bridesmaid (not that she is obsessing over matters fashionista).

We are not thinking too far down the road at present. We have learned to avoid this when immersed in the fullness of difficult treatment. We are unfortunately far too expert at all of this. It would be false pride to pretend that we perfectly cope. Support? We could not imagine living or leading a more supported, prayed for, cared for life. Focus? We could not imagine a greater sense of meaning, Faith, clarity of purpose to our very existence as a family. Blessing? We could not imagine being gifted with more remarkable, loving and lovely children than our two.

But we are sick of me being sick. We need and deserve a serious break from treatment, which just doesn't seem possible. None of this is a challenge to our faith life, our commitment to each other as husband and wife, nor our vision of life's beauty. Last email I promised not to drop any particular bombs, but today I cannot say that. This is more bad news in a two year litany of bad news. But we persist and continue to revel in the small things where life lives: a 12 year old's birthday, curling up as a family and watching an old musical, sugar bread and fresh coffee upon arising on Huron's shore, Henry's daily decision to impart some knowledge upon us that we previously didn't have, and many lovely little instances with family and friends which may be face-to-face or through this strangely effective electronic means.

Until we next communicate, we wish you the same revelry in life's many unsplendoured and often overlooked day-to-day jewels!

Love,
Glenn

> *Consider stippled streaming at day's end*
> *along the line of sky's unending limb*
> *as dusk unfolds with plunging bid of sin*
> *to carry forth the wages past the bend*
>
> *But day breaks clean to rest in sparkling black*
> *which wipes the bloody-rood from memory's sight*
> *So is the deepest cover of good night*
> *to smother over colour on day's back*
>
> *And mother pray to you for your son's way*
> *as dew descends to freshen birthing morn*
> *New day ascends with promise, not forlorn*
> *though shadow lengthens with the hours' decay*
>
> *For freshness comes with bitterness in hand*
> *Life ushers forth eschewing all tinged bland*

September 2, 2009

Dear family,

No bad news here ... we had a decent day in London today. I was hoping that I could stop my nasty IV chemo agent and Dr. W. agreed. I will continue the oral chemo as monotherapy for now. I did receive my IV bone-builder while there. He ordered CT scan of head down to pelvis and hopefully I can arrange this in Cambridge for next week.

I see Dr. H. next Thursday in London to discuss next radiation steps, likely superficial treatment of my face with electrons. There is a chance, depending on the plan and number of treatments, that I could do this in K-W.

We also discussed with Dr. W. future treatment steps of a non-toxic variety if needed.

So, all-in-all, what we were hoping for at this point. We see Dr. W. again in 3 weeks to review all of this discussion. Hopefully I will build some strength in the next weeks now that the nasty one is stopped and add some flesh to my 170 (yikes!) pounds.

Love,
Glenn (& Mary)

September 11, 2009

Dear family,

As I mentioned in last week's email, we met Thursday with our radiation oncologist in London. It was a good, if typically brief, meeting. He wants to move as soon as possible with a radiation plan. In fact, he arranged for me to return to today for "planning" ... further assessment, CT scan, and making the mask.

Mary and I are keen to get going on this, as it does feel that I have plateaued with the chemo treatment, aside from all the nastiness. As it stands, the plan will involve superficial treatment with electrons and likely some very focal deeper treatment, perhaps tomotherapy as I had last winter for the sinus. This will cover a number of tumour sites on my right face. It is only 10 treatments and will start next Tuesday.

We are sticking with London. Too much work to get to know another cancer treatment facility and this sounds like a very manageable number of treatments.

Remember, this is not new news. Ever since my facial biopsies back in June and then the plan for chemo, we have known that further radiation was coming down the road ... much more definitive treatment for my face than the chemo.

That's it for now!

Love,
Glenn & Mary

Dear family,

Believe it or not, time for another update on our status. I know these messages may seem a bit fast and furious over the past couple of months, but such is the nature of the beast ("beast" being the correct metaphor) these days.

Last Monday I finished my current torture, I mean treatment. Actually on the whole it went relatively well – the superficial radiation for my facial and eye lesions. Three or four hours per day for 40 seconds of actual treatment. I asked the therapists if they couldn't just drop by my house with their rad-mobile (like the Bookmobile, or Mary's PAP-mobile), but they declined. You may recall that the end of radiation treatment is not the end of treatment, as the effects perpetuate over the following few weeks, and I certainly feel this, in a generally positive direction.

A little more than two weeks ago I was diagnosed by my chest radiation oncologist (Dr. Y., whom we like even though he seems from a different planet at times) with radiation pneumonitis. This is a relatively common side-effect for those who have received large dose chest rads. It comes as generalized lung inflammation, terrible shortness of breath, cough, mucous, asthma-like symptoms. The treatment is usually high-dose steroids for a few weeks and then a very slow taper over a few months. This is my lot at present. I have benefited greatly from this therapy so far, but the shortness of breath has been a bugger ... patience, patience ... soon I will become too virtuous.

I also recently had full CT scanning from stem-to-stern (head to pelvis) with a difficult mix of results, none shocking for Mary and me. Without resorting to infinitesimal details, my head is a complete mess with tumour effects, boney destruction, inflammation ... makes me feel decent that I have any face left at all (honestly!). Dr. Y. feels that the chest portion is improved, though cannot rule out background carcinomatosis until the pneumonitis clears, i.e. cancer effects may still be present. But, again, we are not expecting full clearing.

I have a single small but suspicious lesion on my liver. Now, hang in there: this is not really qualitatively any different from the seriousness of information we received just before Relay for Life last year with my chest metastases (now 1&1/2 years ago). Dr. H., the problematic-one, has been more responsive lately and will send me to London's top specialist for this. Likely? Watch the lesion since it is not causing problems, and consider stereotactic radiation for the spot.

The CT also showed that there may be more boney spread problems, and Dr. W., our beloved, sent me for a bone scan just this past Friday … no word yet and no rush to that word on our part. We see him after the Thanksgiving weekend.

Again, again, all of this is relatively expected given the sinister nature of my cancer, its aggression. But Dr. W. was just the right tonic last week, as he offered plenty of structure and hope. Our objective is first – time, and second – creative, relatively non-toxic treatment options, and finally – the longish-term window to any sort of miracle, medical or not. Young (I used to be), strong (same) people can live many years with terrible cancer prognoses.

Tomorrow I start on a new biological agent called Tarceva. This is similar to the P-mab I was on last year, but is small-molecule, more varied in its targeting of cancer cells, and lower in side-effects. It is also cheaper and a daily oral dose, which is far preferable to needing IV treatment every few weeks. I will continue on an IV bone builder, which I've been taking since June. But no other chemo at this point. I plan on acquiring some flesh for my bones! I am eating very well and slowly increasing activity to the tolerance of my breathing status.

From a family perspective, we are focused on having some fun. Thanksgiving on the Bruce and then at chez Beingessner next weekend. Mary and I have a few days at the end of the month at the cottage to close up and enjoy the revelry of Autumn. We have a youth choir from Whistler visiting mid-November as the first part of this year's GYS exchange tour. Theo and Lukas will head West at the end of May to complete the visit. Later in November we have tentatively booked a long weekend with Theo and Henry to visit Quebec City, because we deserve to (certainly the kids do, with their utter patience for their invalid father). Then we bash into Advent with a Tactus concert, GYS concert and seasonal festivities … a fabulous time of year for our ritualistic little nuclear-consort!

That is basically it. I think I am due to communicate with the larger audience soon, so you will see that as well (it will be much less specific). I do hold hope that I can rid myself of the need for eye-patching, with which I have a distinct love-hate relationship. It would be nice to have a presentable face, but here I have also learned valuable lessons. As I have said in the past, if I could negotiate my survival, I would not (yes, honestly) give up the cancer experience. Though, I have had enough of it now (vast understatement), and definitely do not recommend it to others!

We are always open to your questions, concerns, gestures and good-will. We are, as always, allergic to pity and despair.

We are blessed by family in all its iterations and thank-you for all you are to us.

Love,
Glenn et al.

IV
Poetry: 2006 B.C.
and Before

Glenn's Credo
(1984)

Glenn was doing some homework for his university courses and listening to music. He came to the kitchen and handed his mother a torn piece of paper with this written on it.

I believe there is a God (and only one God)
     and that It threw Itself
     into human substance and dwelt among us
     and due to unknowable reason
     substituted Its perfect Self
     through sacrifice for our absolute inadequacy
thereby granting us connectedness with the Divine
     in some immediate and yet
     utterly and wholly other way
in both the personal and social dimensions

I believe that Jesus stands infinitely
as our only true model
     in how to live, love each other, and have meaning

I believe the Bible to be an adjunct to this
and to incorporate much Truth
     (though not in any complete sense)

I believe in direct revelation
     that is inexplicable

I believe that I cannot and should not judge the validity of another's
belief in God,
     be he or she Christian,
     Hindu, Buddhist, Islam or Native
     in faith

I believe that God's Love mysteriously surrounds me
And that my maximal understanding of and allowance for it
will not come

       until I do not exist
       in this realm

Lastly,

       I believe that I know nothing more than what I have just stated
       at this particular twinkling of an eye
       in the minuscule monstrosity
we call Time

(I believe that

       I may not even know all that I have just said)

my God is
(November, 1989)

The african sunset (African
sunset) is more ancient
than my god - so I come
to teach the truth to the
Truth.

There was no knowledge in this
dark land before me (there
was no sin in this dark land
before me).

This is the truth (of orange
colours fading into light
across the dimming africa).

And my god - my God - is
here, my inspiration, and
is the african sunset
through me, despite
me, before me.

Praise be to the Dimming Africa.

jp2
(April 3, 2005)

Yesterday the pope died and I don't
    understand the grief
the world seems to show utter
    despair
for the old, crumpled-up man with
    Parkinson's
he of left over intellect – body gone –
    able only to mumble
fallen head – Christ-like on the
    cross – dedicated servant of God

In the end, this most dutiful
    Christian is released
from his decrepit mortal plane
    to the deity
love him or not – agree or disagree
    - he worked hard these 27 years
he owes his followers nothing,
    his legacy in place

Why then all this weeping in Roman
    Christendom?
Should rockets not be set off – a
    celebration of eternal motion –
    a puff of happy smoke?

Forget the tracheostomy –
    Vatican mumbo jumbo –
    medical watchdogs and
    flattened EKGs

The pope is dead!
    Long live the pope!
        Lord, thy servant has
        departed in peace!
            (Hallelujah)

The Day
(April 5, 2005)

      This is the way the day spins out
      This is the way the day spins out
      This is the way the day spins out
      Not with a whimper, but a bang

So I was reflecting upon the Trooper
      and the fact that it did not die
      on the road to Elmira Saturday
      in the whipping wind and sideways
      snow
      with 2 children in back
      and Mennonites dotting the road
      horse and carts at the ready
nor did it die from work to home
      yesterday
      with satchel at my side and day
      at my back
      with long sun and clock change
      and stuporous attention
      imitation at the ready
instead I crept it to the garage
      with gasping breath and
      wheezing exhaust
      to rest until the morning key in
      drop box,
      responsibility transferred
and hitched a ride from nearby
      parents
      with home so soon the day
      not changed

So comes this morning, after evening
      usual

and all the details rear their ugly
> heads:
> sleepy children with clocks unwound
> empty driveway with not a sound
> stressful wife with work impending
> schedules, details never ending
> son with weeping at school's door
> special left home on floor
> daughter slow with piano practice
> spent too long upon her mattress
> this just in from mechanic's call
> used transmission, not quite so tall
> a bill for us this taxing season
> and through the dust I see a reason

to smile and let the details settle
> no one has died, no limbs lost, no tragedy

Shakespeare writes no ode upon our day
> a little one that bangs and clashes
> with our desire for tranquil passage
> through the ordinary of our lives

Indelible Ink
(July 24, 2005)

    veritable Ian Brown mused on his
        summertime's summertimes
    his Rockport Reawakening
    reconnecting with 50's seaside
        archetypes:
        camp, sour sea-smell
        faded HoJo memory
        kitchen table lighthouses
        blonde women toting beach toys
        over-mantel sea-scape paintings
        salty waves at genital height
        the inevitable plunge
        odd, funny reminiscences
    and yet in the emotion of nostalgia
        (the nostalgia of emotion?)
    he fails the weekend reader
        of newspaper drivel
    the prose is flat, prosaically amateur,
        pushed out and predictable
    what of this—our urbane writer
        of TVO fame, erudite, political—
        mind, social-commentator,
        keen-edged pen—
    where is his sardonic muse?

    Remember brain-washed in
        salt-sea air, humidified
        by raunchy clams, freshly
        pickled with 9 year-old thoughts
    the boy Brown of summertime's
        summertime, writing on mildew-
        laced pages of long-forgotten
        notebook, awash in old hormones
        and the rusty barnacles of

images log-jamming the
young mind
we have not lost the 45 year-old
writer of Globe & Mail
we have found the 9 year-old
pre-writer of seaside tale:
of summers lost in foggy dream,
of language trapped regression's mean,
not nasty this, just mundane tomes
of average-ness, with school-aged tones
primary colours, references straight
like rhyming couplet—breezy gate
and if condemned to childhood essays…
we uncouple adult-ness, to the
freedom of "plain-old"-young-Brown
child of salted mind, vacationist from big Town.

(Ref. Globe &Mail; 05.7.23 Focus: "Summertime's 'life indelible")

L. A.
(July 25, 2005)

Armstrong
    ARM-STRONG
Armstrong?
Legstrong
    LEG-STRONG!
Headstrong
Mindstrong
Heartstrong
Willstrong
    STRONG-STRONG!
Dopestrong
       Dope-strong?
       Drugstrong
Medstrong
Test-strong
er-strong
rone-strong
       Cance-strong?
       Lance-strong!
Tourstrong
Windstrong
Winstrong
    ARMSTRONG

(ref. 05.7.25 The Globe & Mail Sports: "Lance—Seven Wins in a row—Armstrong Masters the Gruelling Tours de France")

Terrorism's Terror
(July 26, 2005)

Exposed phone wire transection's threat
Bruce County cell Al Qaeda's net
hidden caves at escarpment's shore
no limestone too thick bombs galore

Blown London tube now Fathom five
deep death-by-drown jihad's alive
no threat too far no place too near
terror's purpose close Lion's Head so clear

The target Bruce no target truce
the end in sight Cape Croker's blight
our cottage shakes pane windows rattle
Pike Bay's the ground mullah's next battle

No safety Harbour's Whiskey still
sobering thoughts invade resolve's will
how can we fight we do not know
Howdenvale's safety suicide's blow

Remove's joke dashes Wiarton's soul
Innocent hearts terror's target (w)hole
Fear creates our present story
None safe Madrid – Tobermory

(July 27, 2005)

Hai

> ku haiku haiku
> haiku haiku haiku hai
> ku haiku haiku

E. T.

> So E. T. phoned home
> The Extraterrestrial
> of glowing finger

Weather

> weather lightens chill
> removes humid's woolen coat
> jacket's breeze refresh

Haiku

> this is a haiku
> properly structured haiku
> a haiku this was

Stress
(July 28, 2005)

funny little thing it is
usually for a price
familiar the agitated sense
best savoured by daylight
      rather than night's embrace

trivial culprit origin
sitting in stomach's pit
despite any larger knowledge
      of another's greater cause

yes, I realize… never helps
if only I could… neither
but look at them…
      and perhaps their plight
      does give a little shape

to the fleeting all-encompassed
of time's heavier feel
paper folly… let it go
no one has died… none sick
      … no loss or tragedy
and yet it lingers past its stay
      familiar uninvited

Gin's Tonic
(July 29, 2005)

juniper bush gives up its ghost
      to open up the view
great Huron calls, its wide expanse
      revealed as something new

we fuss and strain o'er labour's cost
      when lapping shores are blue
with water's beauty not by chance
      that gives us life's big clue

'tis not the roses smell the most
      but rather morning's dew
upon the cedars' green romance
      to junipers so pooh pooh!

your berries to we raise a toast
      though nature gives her cue
gnarled roots we chop so when we glance
      lake's view comes through so true!

(a corny ode to juniper excavation at the cottage)

Buxtehude Blues (1705)
(July 30, 2005)

late night stupor
     unfocused mind
     black-blue sky with crickets' song
chirpy continuo to Buxtehude's lament
"must death set free as Adam's fall
     cannot?"

daylight's death sets free evening's mind
     black-blue rainbow unfolds concentration
     strophic song in somber mood
gentle basso pushes on
mind wanders forward

does Buxtehude belong on Huron's
     summer shore?
     three-hundred years since Bach's
     famous walk
     would JS have sojourned here
     for reedy organ music
     thinly piped from little black-blue
     box on Huron's shelf?
Adam's fall sits down with cricket continuo
stuporous journey of wandering mind
midnight's unfocus

Coffee's Brew
(July 31, 2005)

coffee's brew upon my nose, as fresh as
     morning's dew
lightly up upon my lips, this morning's
     starting cup
banished mind from dream's travails,
     coffee's cup so kind
once again the day begins, elixir of
     good men

coffee's true upon my brain,
     invigoration's clue
boldened cup upon my heart, the
     day is moving up
strengthened spine for day's big deeds
     all from coffee's grind
good for Glenn this blackened gold,
     must go it's half past ten!

Katrina's Coup
(sky-high)
(September 3, 2005)

Hurricane's power
Katrina's finite shower
Division's hour

Police state's glower
Black-and-white Babel's tower
Fetid eyes' cower

Slime's fertile bower
New Orleans' toxic chowder
Nature's sad flower

Silly Late Evening Evolving Poem
(September 25, 2005)

I am writing this silly little poem
        as the clock strikes twelve
        and my head begins to
        swim with sleep
Did you know "poetry" is an
        acronym for people-of-every-
        type-rhyme-yet?

Sleep swims silently around me
        and yet I sit with silly
        stanzas slipping through my
        semi-consciousness
Did you know "sleep" is an
        acronym for silly-little-
        eye-energy-pause?

Poems dip through silly sleepy
        syllables as the clock ticks
        past twelve and yet
        my eyes seem slightly open
Did you know "clock" is an
        acronym for continuous-
        little-operating-click-kiss
                        Good-night!

Jesus loves – this I know
(October 7, 2005)

"We strive to love the way Jesus did"
(Dublin church Core Values 2005)

And so we sit on the precipice of
    our decision ... as always
comfortable ground, this in-between
    avoiding past conflict and
    future commitment

But the present-tense is real,
    alive, happening now ... we strive
not we will, we should, we did
    but we do
    strive in present-tense

And so tension sits with us on
    this precipice ... we are
conflicted people, by definition
    we contradict ourselves
    bring our singular disarray
    to the group

Our community is this muddled collection
    of real people, faithful ... bound by
one example in flesh of Love and Spirit
    co-opted together
    so that we may learn the
        good decision
        alone and communing

The Creator creates the model
    of us ... for us
to strive in love, with love
    and for Love

for nothing else – not judgment
nor wealth, nor power

We are not called to be vacuous
or lukewarm ... or indecisive
but we are charged by Love
with love to love
and if we err
(and we will)
are we to err on the side of judgment?
or do we err on the side of love?

And so we sit at a precipice ...
(judgment spares no victims)
let us follow Love,
our Lord ... our love
let us err in love

Claudia of cherubic grace

on her baptism
(October 15, 2005)

Claudia of cherubic grace
      peaceful spirit upon thy face
thou hast wisdom of divine space
      God's infant new to human place

Grant that this water's holy splash
      upon thy forehead - dripping lash
given baptism's sacred wash
      now girded in the Spirit's sash

Gaze calmly on the gathered throng
      thine eyes speak clear thine heart is strong
great gathered love thy soul drinks long
      our hallowed prayers to amen song

So good Claudia we bid you
      peace and justice that come to few
yet more we strive for thy life new
      may God's great joy colour thy view

Thy days will smile with Spirit's grace
      Love's countenance upon thy face
thy life will fill with light and space
      God's child thou are in any place

When forty winters besiege thy brow
(Shakespeare's Sonnet #2) for Jessica
October 22, 2005

As forty years have sculpt thy face
  so to thy life time brings her grace
and sculptor's hands from clay do mould
  object beauty for use, to hold
cherish, lovely from thy caress
  these years upon thine art do bless

No furrowed brow doth time display
  as sun moveth from day to day
thine art, thy muse, thy vital spark
  fair Jessica of Av'nue Park
thy home of brick from stone is made
  Hauser's Stein, thy gift shan't fade

As forty more do etch thy face
  so too thine hands with sculptor's grace
will ply thy trade, thy gift so bold
  we friends lay claim our hearts enfold
round thine art, we warmly cherish
  thy birth's day many more we wish!

Auntie Meg
(March 9, 2006)

When death comes, it seems
    extraordinary
And yet for others – Victorians,
    Georgians, the Enlightened,
    Medievals, and before –
    death was ordinary, expected

We have divorced ourselves from
    expectation
death is rare, unexpected,
    unintended, preventable,
    uninvited

We embrace our longevity, our
    teflon-coated existence, our
    very permanence
And yet for others, death was
    around every corner,
    inevitable, accepted

Only we are separated, have
    separated from it, only
    our age is disconnected
    from it

(It
it
death
Death)

And so we are shocked, appalled
    by the diagnosis, prognosis
    by its immediacy, closeness
    its lack of structure

its open emptiness
its terminality, finality

In the midst of life, we are
        in death

It surrounds us, gently waiting
        birth in and birth out
        breathe in, breathe out
        don't breathe, stop breath
        stop and birth out of life
        out of breath
        out of life
        out of time
timelessness
death's time

At the end of life, we are
        in death

It waits knowing
        that we live in false hope
        of avoiding it

And yet it waits, unconcerned
        with expectation, unconcerned
        with invitation, just ordinary it

It is the unseen guest that
        always walks alongside life
        always faithful, never late
                nor early

It comes always
        in the midst of life

On the kiss of her lips
       she whispers Jesus
the invitation given
fullest expectation
the closeness of It
heart's desire
she embraces death
              birth out

Katerjina

{a sonnet deconstructed}

(June 6, 2006)

So fifty winters have besieged thy brow, my dear
yet thy beauty's field buds with new growth, gently tilled
all that was you folds into what you will yet become
my dear, nary a weed nor tattered foliage at that

If being asked where all thy beauty lies
you would demure, I know
not looking backward upon earlier days
nor seeking the affirmation of empty praise

But I will speak of beauty on thy behalf, praise deserved
for along these years I have observed your hands
with grace of purpose and gifted touch
dispense much beauty to singer's phrase or keyboard's song

For, if I may, in those hands of yours, my dear
fifty winters do warm with beauty's flow, and thine art's pulse

for Catherine, on the occasion of her 50th birthday
with a direct nod to Shakespeare's Second Sonnet:

When forty winters shall besiege thy brow,
And dig deep trenches in thy beauty's field,
Thy youth's proud livery, so gazed on now,
Will be a tatter'd weed, of small worth held:
Then being ask'd where all thy beauty lies,
Where all the treasure of thy lusty days,
To say, within thine own deep-sunken eyes,
Were an all-eating shame and thriftless praise.
How much more praise deserved thy beauty's use,
If thou couldst answer 'This fair child of mine
Shall sum my count and make my old excuse,'

Proving his beauty by succession thine!
This were to be new made when thou art old,
And see thy blood warm when thou feel'st it cold.

Prose: 2006 B.C.
and Before

Room 340, Moose Factory General Hospital
P.O. Box 34, Moose Factory, Ont. P0L 1W0
November 27, 1988

Dear Mum and Dad,

What a wonderful and varied experience this is and will prove to be. I use the work "wonderful" in its most literal sense - I am full of wonder in almost all that I experience here (paper and pen cannot do descriptive justice to this), but most of all I am full of wonder at how I feel in this place. I feel incredibly "alive" through the bulk of my days here.

We arrived securely and fatigued around noon on Thursday. The accommodations provided us are most pleasant, tidy and private. We are situated on the third floor of the hospital, with the second floor consisting of wards and O.R. and the first composed mainly of the out-patient department, administration, labs, and cafeteria (which serves good and substantial meals). The afternoon was ours for rest and a stroll through the mud to the Hudson's Bay Company, which happens to be the second one ever established (1672... pre-Bach's birth). Three hundred years' existence has resulted in an entirely unimpressive and yet quite meaningfully impressive structure and business (paradoxes do abound in the mooseless island of Moose Factory, where the tourists come in the short height of summer by Polar Bear Express to Moosonee, a town 200 miles south of the northern polar bear, so that they may experience the North American Indian (there's a very good paradox) culture where most crafts are imported from Quebec or Winnipeg while the governmentally established native territory has its health care needs met by the "pair" of "docs" staffing the hospital which is the sole industry on the island). I'm glad that's out of my rectum. When I say that there is a tremendous amount of beautiful injustice here, I do so only because within this environment I can and do breathe some sort of fresh and utterly different air which I do not fully understand at present. Perhaps I will understand a little more when I leave this holy and richly historical land and head home. Perhaps I will understand better that the ground upon which I commonly tread is wholly and wrongfully mine. Perhaps I will love Adrian, whose brother and guest I am, a little more and a little differently. Perhaps I will never listen to the Bach to which

I am listening now in the same way again. Perhaps I will just breathe the same old, stale air again, just like before. Perhaps I will take this absolute lack of understanding of this place and of my being and plunge deeper into the truth of faith and its consequences.

Ah, well, to the mundane and the descriptive once more: where am I? I didn't quite complete Thursday and am limited by space (and time - in the ontological sense, of course). I had intended to describe my four days in detail thus far, but will summarize relation of the facts involved. We have been given great deal of flexibility by the medical director who feels our experience of Cree culture to be of equal importance to clinical experience. Friday night I was invited by one of the doctors to sing some Beatles' songs with his band (which includes other doctors and nurses). Saturday Joanne, John (a clinical clerk from Queen's), and I took motorized canoe to Moosonee for our interesting tour around. In the evening, I played pictionary with a bunch of the doctors...blah, blah, blah...went to church today...blah, blah... going to fly an elderly dying patient up the western coast to Peawanuck (formerly Minick) tomorrow...snow storm today.

Love,
Glenn

POSTCARD

Moose Factory
November 30, 1988

Dear Mum and Dad,

What a very strange day it is today. It is profoundly gray outside with light snowfall. A sombre melancholia covers the hospital. Yesterday the pediatrics ward was spilling over with kids from all over. A team from Queen's was up for assessment of slowly developing kids. Today the ward is empty. Little, but important, medical problems are the order of the day from neonatology to geriatrics. The focus for the "grayness" is unfortunately in the form of fatality. Two pilots and two paramedics were killed last night on their way to Chapleau for medivac. This has raised much sadness and anxiety, since anyone here could conceivably have been on that trip. Northern medicine has very many different twists involved with it. Our trip to Moosonee last Saturday is pictured on the front of this card. It was mild with very little snow on the ground when we came, but since the storm Saturday and Sunday the river has frozen (hence, no more boat travel) and cross-country skiing is in full swing. I remain quite enamoured with the stark beauty and cold reality of this environment. I will write again soon re more descriptions (especially with regard to trip this past Monday).

December 9, 1988

Dear Mum,

My time here continues to be splashed with many meaningful moments. What an enjoyable experience it was to read your neatly composed letter - a sure contrast to Dad's perfected cursory style. I am writing with headphones and King's College Choir service of lessons and carols in place. It is terribly easy to become inspired here. I suppose you can have 2 C.D.'s playing at the same time now (I am mildly flabbergasted). Pediatric rounds held no inspiration for me this morning, so here I sit composing letters while sparkles of muted sunlight enter my room through a frosted window pane. I am now able to redefine coldness. The past two nights have -25 to -30 C. And to get quite abstract - many Platonic forms are more closely approximated in the bleak midwinter of Moose Factory. Gitchi Manitou or (Cree word) is readily palpable in the midst of singing Christmas carols in Cree.

On the slightly less esoteric plane, I have some suggestions for the furtherance of your ideas around what you would aspire to purchase for me with regard to Christmas: 2-3 dress shirts (one white with button down collar, others with stripes), bathrobe, chess set, 1-2 ties (do you think silk in nice?). These are only suggestions and may be completely disregarded.

I am attempting to integrate myself into the community here as much as is possible when one is staying for one month and is white. Tonight I will join the church choir (which is almost all native) in carolling throughout the hospital and then for a pot-luck. I appreciated your supportive and loving words and feel warmly secure in the cold of MF.

Love,
Glenn

General Hospital
Moose Factory, Ontario
December 12, 1988

Dear Mum and Dad,

This is my last letter and I'm afraid a rushed on, as I leave for Atawapiskat in 20 minutes. Even though my ideas of communication were destroyed last night, it was still relatively nice to hear your voices from the south. I don't really feel that this is north any more, but do feel that I must go north in the not too distant future. There is much to explore, both externally and internally, as one heads north and I believe much still lies in waiting for me. Perhaps the concept of migrating north will be a strong theme in the narrative of my life. Certainly the element of native culture in some form or other (that is to say, "yet to be determined or shared") will be incorporated and woven into the footsteps I take from Moose Factory onwards.

There is so much I could still write; but there is also so much that I cannot put into words. I do feel blessed, however, in having parents with whom I can openly share some of that which comes from deep within (or more likely from deep without in terms of the divine origins of the most personal thoughts and feelings).

I could describe church services, the weather, coastal trips, the people I have met and worked with, the volleyball tournament in which I participated (reflecting upon which I will record sometime soon), but I don't really feel like it nor do I have time.

I think it important, though, to encourage the idea of a trip to experience the northern native culture for the two of you. I would do so with Becky and Monica as well. Certainly I eagerly anticipate visiting and working in Europe in the new year. And I look forward to the possibility of studying overseas and working in a 3rd world country someday. But, in terms of personal meaning, the experience I have had here in Moose Factory will and must remain the most important.

Last night I sang a couple of solos at the service of lessons and carols at St. Thomas Anglican church (refer to Dad's card). One was "'Twas in the Moon of Wintertime", which presents a very accessible, ecumenical, cross-cultural, universal and Platonic archetypal view of (Cree word) (there, that extinguishes my reservoir of adjectives). "O Little Town of Moose Factory, how still we see thee lie..." As the day when we celebrate the incarnation of meaning fast approaches, so I will be home soon to spend another salient Christmas with my weird and wonderful family.

Love,
Glenn

(postcard sent from London, while beginning elective to St. Oswald's Hospice, Newcastle-upon-Tyne-London, Westminster Cathedral)
89.03.20

Dear Mum, Dad and everyone,

It has begun so quickly, so suddenly. The London sky is crystal blue and a damp radiance fills my first perceptions of the city. And yet I sit as quietly as possible inside this very cathedral.

My plane landed but 3 hours ago and already I have discovered a beautiful bleakness (in here - this blackened, ornamented, post-Reformation anachronism). A shaft of light stabs through the stained ceiling to illuminate the figure of Truth - Christ stands universal again in the "Catholicism" of an Anglican land, Truth abounds. I am not tired even with less than 2 hours sleep). I discussed linguistics with a francophone professor, who was coming to present a paper, during the trip.

My journey has begun - I will attend services here this afternoon.

Love,
Glenn

St. Oswald's Hospice
Regent Avenue
Newcastle-upon-Tyne
England, U.K.
NE3 1EE
89.04.01

Dear Mum and Dad,

I thought it was time to write again, having finished my week in London and my first week in Newcastle. First, the address you have for me is absolutely correct. There is some excellent accommodation provided within this beautiful hospice. The front of this card shows the conservatory which surrounds an inner cloister. The hospice is two and a half years old and its design was selected through a national architectural competition. The building has since gone on to win a national architectural award.

I would like to summarize my memorable and hectic week in London for you before proceeding to answer some of your questions with regard to St. Oswald's (if present space permits). I have accommodated and acclimatized quite well to England, though the clocks went forward an hour last Saturday. I can't remember when we "spring forward" back home, so I may be 6 hours ahead of you for the time being.

I bought along 2 guide books to England from home and didn't use them while in London. Last night I sat down and read through their London sections and was amazed to discover that I had basically encapsulated their recommendations for capturing London. These experts, however, suggested that the traveller should select a narrow region for discovery unless prepared for an extended stay. The structure of my journey was, of course, sculpted according to what was personally meaningful rather than standard tourist fair. On average, I spent over 12 hours per day in central London exploring. The transit system is easily manageable with a week-long pass covering tube, bus, and rail travel according to certain zones. My accommodation was SE of central London (S of the Thames) and a 20 minute trip by train. The McGeorges were away my entire stay except for the evening of the day I arrived when Mr. McGeorge met me before heading to his work at Southampton and then to meet his family at their cottage in Cornwall. It was very strange to enter the country and be given an empty house. The arrangements suited me well and the McGeorges appreciated a house-sitter for the week (they were burgled over Christmas by a federal agency, he hypothesizes). The location of this house was in Maze Hill, which is adjacent to Greenwich. Henry VIII's observatory was down the street from me, though I didn't get a chance to explore it.

The pace in London is quite mad! There are many nationalities and too many people - though the Easter holiday may have caused an exacerbation. The city, which is a city made of various cities, is quite filthy, unfortunately. Part of my daily routing (ritual?) was to return home after a long day and promptly blow soot out of my nose (and there was none-too-little).

London is also terribly "smashing" in all of its richly-textured dimensions. My journey was sewn together by an ongoing narrative interwoven with soliloquies inspired according to the impact of my particular environment. The downfall of travelling alone and not being able to converse and share with a companion becomes pale when compared with the colours strewn throughout the developing tapestry of this journey. Enough metaphorical writing (though perhaps this is a journey laden with metaphors - can such a journey exist without such?)

89.04.02

Londoners, on the whole, seem a rather cold lot. The natives of Newcastle instantaneously impressed me with their friendliness, by contrast. England is a country laden with hierarchies, whether it be from the snobbery of the South to the openness of the North, within its labourious and tremendously tiered medical system, the gradations between economic classes, or the various political levels governed by the asexual autocrat. Nonetheless, it continually strikes me with the fullness of its history and the depth of its arts. I believe that in many ways it is more a country that was than is. I have also discovered a strangely building conviction that I am Canadian and will continue to be so and that this is good (very good indeed). This holds no ramifications for the possibility of doing a PhD at Cambridge or for living here and there now and then (whether it be the planet Earth or not; I should not restrict myself at present). By the way, I have not visited Cambridge yet, but will some coming weekend and also hope to get to Birmingham.

Another discovery is that I am rather obsessed with completeness - which as an abstract concept, in the Platonic sense, can be very productive, but in practice may prove harrowing, especially if travelling independently. I have always possessed this obsession; it has just come home to me quite clearly in my approach to this journey. Travelling alone has provided me the privilege of covering much territory and I must now get more descriptive. This is a long letter.

My first day in London was extremely long as I did not arrive at the McGeorges' until about midnight and didn't get off to bed before 1 a.m. (a flavour of what is to come when I return to surgery). This may be a good way of dealing with jet lag, however, i.e., establishing yourself according to the time of your destination and not sleeping until it is appropriate. I write you a card from my first meaningful discovery - Westminster Cathedral (CD reference: 2 motets and masses by Victoria - in particular motet "O Magnum Mysterium"). From there I ate a steak and kidney pie and began to walk with my handy-dandy map in hand (the perfect and sufficient tour guide for 50p). I quickly discovered Westminster Abbey, Big Ben, and the Parliament Buildings. There was a booth outside the Abbey advertising the sale of tickets for a concert that very evening (Monday, March 20) by the choir (CD reference: 2 Handel CD's that are well known already). So I purchased my ticket, not having contacted my billet as yet nor knowing whether the trains would run out to Maze Hill late. The concert's main works were the Faure Requiem and Allegri's Misere. I was stunned by the appropriateness of this for my introductory concert in London during Holy week. (CD reference: Taverner Consort recording Allegri, your recording of Allegri by KKC; record/tape reference: John Rutter recording of Faure, the tape of my performance of both). It was then that I caught the full force of the vims - you are of course worried, but this is pleasing pathology. I must search for music. I incurred a ravenous appetite that could not be cured - satiation was impossible. I quickly sought out advice regarding the best network for gaining information about concerts and in particular early music. I had one address in hand already from Gramophone magazine and had little problem pursuing others.

Thus, the afternoon of this huge first day was spent casing as much of central London as I could on foot. I visited the Westminster library and St. John's Smith Square (a favourite place for recording, reference CD's) with regard to my music network, visited the Westminster bridge and the Thames, visited Trafalgar Square and the National Gallery, Lord Nelson, St. Martin-in-the-Fields, visited St. James's Park and Buckingham Palace, visited St. Luke's church in Chelsea regarding tickets for a Tuesday night concert, and then headed back to Westminster Cathedral for Vespers and was surrounded by incense flickering through the shadows as the male voices of the choir sang chant and motets by Palestrina, lulling me gently into a late afternoon semiconsciousness as the high blue sky and radiant sun were replaced by a cold, wet wind. So I picked up my body and carried it to Westminster Abbey for my first concert. I sat my weary self down, contentedly, in my same smelly attire of some 30 hours and in the midst of the well-clad English. The choir silently processed out in their red, and it was then that I noticed the Allegri Miserere in the program, having foreknowledge and of the Faure. I smiled silently to myself and absorbed the music as it floated by my heavy head. In retrospect, it was oppressive - the weight of the music and history mingled in the acoustic of the Abbey, where coronations, royal weddings and burials exist, where Henry Purcell and Handel made glorious music and lie buried, where monks lived and ruled Christianity and occasionally the politics of all England...I returned to Victoria Station, retrieved my luggage after contacting Mr.McGeorge, found the proper train connection, dragged my luggage up Maze Hill in the buckets of rain, drank some lukewarm tea filled with creamy milk and discussed mystery, bathed in tepid water, and slept deeply.

I must go to sleep now. It is just past midnight on the Sunday after Easter. I will finish this horrendous letter tomorrow with much brevity (I hope). Perhaps I am writing this short story as much for my own indulgence as for your information.

89.04.03

I arrived in London in the early afternoon Tuesday, as my sleep was a long and much needed one. It was exciting to approach the city with a fresh mind and body. St. Paul's, the Tower Bridge, and the Tower of London were all visible on the train ride in. You asked what my biggest thrill was in London and I don't think there was one such thrill. Perhaps the unrealistic sense of wonder as I gazed face-to-face with the wonderful historical structures is the closest approximation. This is probably untrue, however, as the wonder of such experiences fits quietly into the fabric of my first week's journey in view of the case with which I soon travelled around the city and my confidence in the knowledge of what I desired to capture and in my ability to do so. My mindset and framework and attitude for the week were quickly established. I investigated Piccadilly Circus and the theatres of Leicester Square in the afternoon, then grabbed a quick bite nearby. London is very expensive and I opted for 2 meals a day for financial reasons - this proved no great burden. I enquired around and found cheap, quality places for feed. I then headed for my concert at St. Luke's: The Hilliard Ensemble, and, of course, its primary tenor Rogers Covey-Crump (many CD references). The performance was of "Passio", a modern St. John Passion composed by Arvo Part, a thought-provoking and spine-tingling Estonian composer. This stood in perfect continuity with my Holy Week mindset. It was also the first of 3 St. John Passions I heard during the week.

Wednesday began with a visit to the South Bank Centre, home of the Royal Philharmonic Orchestra, 3 contrasting concert halls, and a wonderful gallery. "Brilliant", like "smashing", is a common adjective used in this country and certainly applies to the Leonardo da Vinci exhibit at the Hayward Gallery, not to mention the entirety of my week. I witnessed many of Leonardo's most important sketches, including anatomical ones. Absolutely extraordinary!

I forgot to mention that I ran upstairs to the gallery in the House of Parliament after the concert Tuesday evening and spent 10 minutes watching some boring live politics as they hadn't shut down for the long-winded day. Back to Wednesday.

The afternoon was spent exploring Oxford Street (quite amazing), the world class HMV CD shops (as per Gramophone information), and a good centre for early music, Wigmore Hall (as per Gramophone information - in fact, I could have set my travel agenda according to this all important periodical). I then bused to the Palace Theatre and queued for return tickets to "Les Miserables" (thinking very much about Monica's experience). At 7:00 p.m., after standing in line for 3 hours, I got "me" tickets, grabbed a mouthful, and then sat down and was increasingly moved by this production.

Thursday began with the changing of the guard at Buckingham. Liz invited me in to watch from the front bay window. I graciously declined and offered my inside spot to a pregnant 87 year old hag with no limbs and her head screwed on backwards. (She had given me her seat earlier on the tube.) My height was an advantage in peering over the "foreign mass" - in a different system, some sort of chemotherapy would be used to treat this condition. Everyone in this silly mass of people was snapping yards of photos. I do hope mine turn out OK. Have you noticed that every now and then a word appears clearer than the rest of this scratch? Neither have eye, but I thought it time to insert a question. Mind you, "chemotherapy" or chemotherapy looks more distinct than the rest, perhaps due to the clear wit involved with the comment above. Are you still with me? Where am I? I am slipping into profound absurdity and must catch hold of another stream of consciousness. "Catch hold", of course, refers to the imbibing of a large and filling (the ultimate compliment) meal (or bucket of concrete) in the native vernacular (written clearly and hopefully spelled correctly). I do miss a dictionary when writing. I have not found the proper stream as yet and am using the 1st person pronoun I at the beginning of many recent sentences. I used "the" 2 times the last proper sentence. I am not using any new or old drugs, though there is plenty of morphine available downstairs. I don't know why my mind is doing this. I have not undergone some psychotic conversion reaction due to the deaths of patients in the hospice. I am finished this paragraph.

I should admit that I drank some Guinness (black, black, ale) earlier this evening at the expense of a nurse tutor visiting the hospice for 2 weeks from Devon. I hated it and knew that I would. We shared in a good conversation even though the half pint was wasted along with is quid. Back to Thursday, finally. I toured Westminster Abbey in the afternoon - what incredible and thick history! I just finished a little book called "Britain's Kings and Queens" two days ago and can fit much of its information into my memories from Westminster. I then quickly checked out the British Museum and headed for my first trip to St. Paul's. Absolutely Impressive and Awe-Inspiring! I should mention, however, that although the power and dominant impression of St. Paul's is without rival, Westminster Abbey holds my fascination. My plans for Easter weekend were solidly forming (CD reference: St. Paul's choir "My Spirit Hath Rejoiced"). Afterwards, I headed west and checked out the Royal Opera House at Covent Garden and its neighbouring territory. I played with the idea of attending another theatre performance, but opted for the economically pleasing and restful evening of tele watching and a chat over the phone with Stephen Farmer.

Once again I retire to bed leaving this monumental beast unfinished

89.04.04

Back for what must be my final instalment - these midnight letter writings are becoming too habitual. Speaking of open houses, I've just finished my most glorious evening in Newcastle thus far. (I realize that this last sentence is not parallel, but it is effective regardless of syntax.) I attended my first ever operatic performance: Mozart's "Don Giovanni". The production was staged by the Scottish National Opera at Newcastle's newly refurbished Theatre Royal, which is a grand opera house in high Victorian style. I was quite captivated (record reference: "Amadeus" excerpts from the opera). I must return to and finish my London segment of the journey before detailing Newcastle at a later date.

My Good Friday worship I have already detailed in a card written during the evening performance of Bach's SJP. The second SJP of my week transpired earlier in the day (I don't think I mentioned this in the postcard) at the morning service at the Abbey. It was a setting by Victoria. The first three hours of the afternoon consisted of the introspective and meditative service based on Christ's seven last words from the Cross in scripture, string quartet, and hymn selections with appropriate and rather inspiring and challenging and loving thematic messages from the Dean of St. Paul's. The acoustic allowed you to savour the various elements of the service just that little, holy bit longer. I grabbed a bite and returned for evensong, which the choir began with Lotti's excruciating "Crucifixus". The evening was a quick steak and kidney pie at Trafalgar Square and Bach in St. Martin's. It was a good, though not excellent, performance by up-and-coming, raw and talented younger "authenticists". That work continues to retain much meaning for me. The only element lacking in my Holy week celebrations and meditations was my own component of singing in performance. This, of course, must wait until I am finished medical training (or at least further along then I am at present).

I received your second correspondence today and it was much appreciated. It sounds like a meaningful weekend was had by all back at home. Both Friday and Sunday sounded beautifully salient. Whether in London, England, or in Emo or in blackness, the resurrected Word must bring meaning. The setting and structure of our celebrations is absolutely second to our recognition of Truth incarnate, killed, buried and eternally rebirthed. Adrian's sports update is eternally appreciated, though in actuality he was just obeying orders. I expect another such update soon (especially since the NCAA championship was last night!) As sickening as it may seem, I've gone and introduced the goofball to many people here through various relevant conversations. Pretty soon I'll have to have "I'm Adrian's Brother" tattooed on my forehead, though I think that inscription more pertinent to the area on which I presently sit. Actually, it is quite nauseating how often I mention each and every individual in my family to others because of the unique and blessed attributes of each individual's existence.

Let's get this letter finished! This is the last piece of paper in this pad. Saturday consisted of a visit to Harrods, which is a place of great scandal in the news here at present, and a tour through Hyde Park. Harrods is unbelievable, especially the wall-to-wall customers. I could not stand the pushing long and found the park a much needed change in people density. I then grabbed the tube and made my long awaited trip to the Tower of London. I joined one of the Beefeater-guided tours and was spellbound by his storytelling abilities and the sheer history of the place. The line-up for a gaze at the Royal jewels was, without exaggeration, over 2 hours long, so I gave up on the glittery experience. After running around for a while, until the Tower was 30 minutes from its close, I noticed a relatively short queue and got a good look at the stones - I am very glad I did. I then hit my favourite restaurant and attended a concert at the South Bank Centre of Telemann's "St. Matthew Passion"; a wonderful performance by a wonderful authentic group, the St. James' Baroque Players, composed of many of my favourite performers from recordings (CD reference: my Baroque and Renaissance collection). Telemann was not, is not, and will never be Bach, however!

Easter Sunday was gloriously warm and brilliantly sunny and utterly appropriate. I missed the beginning of the first service at St. Paul's Matins, due to an error in alarm setting, even though I had successfully forwarded the clock. The following eucharist was magnificent, with Byrd's "Anec Dies", Mozart's "Coronation Mass" and simple and personal communion. I then visited the Museum of London, which is a wonderful exhibit capturing stone age, Roman, Norman, Medieval, reformation, Victorian, and modern London. There isn't much else to capture, unless historical exhibits of the future were displayed. I find Roman London the most fascinating, with the London of the plague and Dickens and Pepys and Charles II and the Great Fire next, and the London of the Blitzkrieg also quite interesting. After this information-packed hour, I headed to Westminster Cathedral for evening prayer and benediction with steaming incense, shafts of light slicing through its darkness, and Palestrina. Having come full circle (a little "completion"), I left rather transported and spent the remainder of the afternoon at the national Gallery. Ottawa may have a beautiful building; but it needs paintings. I was particularly engrossed by Rembrandt. I witnessed a few pieces that I had studied in Kenneth Clark's book Civilization and dabbled in some very old stuff and the impressionist masters - Monet, van Gogh (van you gotta go, you've got to Gogh), Degas, Matisse, and Cezanne...A quick organ recital at Westminster Abbey and then I headed south over the Themes to the South Bank centre for a perfect denouement: Monteverdi's "Vespers of 1610" with early mucisianists of the highest order, namely the Gabrielli Consort and His Majesty's Sagbutts and Cornets (CD references: Monteverdi "Vespers" (my version very similar to the performance) and your "Orfeo and Eurydice" for the latter group (as well as Schutz "Mysicalische Exgriuen" of mine); also my Rutter CD has "Haed Dies" on it). It was a performance above satisfaction. I packed my bags contentedly, dragged them down to the Victoria Coach Station on Monday, and crammed myself on the second deck of a bus to Newcastle for 5 hours.

What a privilege and blessing was (is) that eventful week. Goodnight and Goodbye.

Love,
Glenn

France
89.05.04

Bonjour ma famille,

Je suis dans France at j'ai un tres bon temps. Il fait tres chaud avec beaucoup de soleil. Hier, nous arrivons a Nancy apres Reims et Paris. Vous excusez mon grammar en francais s'il vous plait. C'est amusant to bastardize la langue francaise. Paris est une grande ville avec beaucoup do personnes. J'arrive a Paris Samedi par l'autobus depuis Newcastle a London, et depuis London a Paris audessus de soir avec une voyage de ferry entre. J'arrive a Paris a sept heures at demi avec beaucoup de fatigue parceque l'autobus est ne conducive pas pour un bon journey.

I must tell you about my Newcastle time, though, before relating any details of my journey through France thus far (I must mention, however, that le vin francais est tres bon). France is wonderful, London was tremendous, but Newcastle was and is special - in the purest and most personal sense of the word. London was very difficult to capture on paper, but I felt satisfied in my attempt. My experience in Newcastle will be utterly impossible. The deepest things cannot be said and certainly cannot be written - though there exist meaningful statements or utterances that are more easily communicated on paper than by word of mouth (this, however, may be more a matter of comfort than of appropriateness of the medium for speaking and expressing). But my pleasant dilemma is, as always and in approximation, the Kierkegaardian one - the core of my experience in Newcastle, like my experience in Moose Factory, is simple mine. It is perfectly subjective.

Both my Moose Factory and Newcastle electives were crucial for many different reasons, but my experience in England has certainly presented a broader scope of meaning for me. This may translate more concretely with regard to my future goals and achievements, but with no more influence on my narrative than the immediacy and simple significance of the Canadian north. My obtuse evaluation of the Newcastle experience should be under¬stood as being nothing but complimentary. It is time for some detail and for me to interrupt this letter to pursue le jour, le soleil, l'histoire, at la musique de Nancy - a bientot!

89.05.05

Bonjour!

C'est un autre bon jour dans la countryside de Nancy. J'ecrie apres mon petit diner de matin - les repas francaise est tres distinctive. Il est dix heures at cinze.

I must post this letter today in the hope that it will precede my arrival in Canada - but I have so much to relate. (This is, however, a blessing rather than a burden.) I cannot believe that I will be home in one week. In many ways, I do not want to believe this. It seems that I have been away only momentarily, not because my last time home feels recent, but rather due to my complete involvement with all of the environments during my journey. When everything, literally every thing, is novel, time loses its place and perceptibility, with the exception of sleep (basic biological needs ground us quite firmly to this earth at les toilettes - excuse moi, le gastrocolic reflex beckons).

Je retourne at ceva bien. Perhaps there is a component of this strange timelessness involved with eternity. Perhaps eternal perception is consistently novel and outside the parameters of time. Perhaps God is having a nice little post-lunch chuckle about this analogy - he/she/it is a few hours ahead of our time zone I believe. So we continue to live day-to-day, incorporating our past, present, and future into our every moment, and always struggling to grasp the eternal concept. All hypothesizing aside, however, heaven must have green pastures such as those before me now.

I arrived in Newcastle 5 Mondays (Lundis) ago and spent my first week acclimatizing with the staff and medical director Claud Regnard, as Kathryn Mannix was on holiday (which I knew beforehand). Claud is a wonderful, humorous, short, and gifted man who is terribly busy and gave me much of his time. The staff from top to bottom, or from side-to-side, as the hierarchy is quite flattened at the hospice, are wonderfully varied and consistently full of life. It was a delightful oxymoron to experience - people full of life working in palliative care. I gained a good sense of the hospice's philosophy and work but was very unsure of my role after one week. I was also very unsure as to whether Kathryn and I would interact on the same plane as Claud and I did. The Saturday of my first weekend was spent exploring Newcastle and working my territory - peeing in all the corners, so to speak. Sunday, I attended a high Anglican service in a small community near Gosforth, where the hospice is located, with a bunch of old people. In the afternoon I travelled a half-hour by metro to a grotty, as the natives would say, industrial district called Jarrow. Here, surrounded by some sort of refinery stands the venerable Bede's church and the remains of his monastery - St. Paul's. This insignificant looking church from the 7th C. is one of the most significant churches in all of Britain. I was stunned to learn of the importance of the NE of England and specifically ancient Northumbria in the history of Christianity and of England. This area was the crucible in which Roman and Celtic Christianity met and then developed. This extraordinary! Above all, I have found this history immensely salient in the most personal dimension. I have a choice between finishing this letter toute de suite or not compromising myself and finishing it later with the distinct possibilite that it will arrive apres moi.

a bientot

(Later, on that same day...)

For your collective information, I am now using a black pen, as my blue one has run dry. I, on the other hand, am still running high and will change my tact in this letter. Instead of proceeding, or plodding, in chronological fashion, I will attempt to capture my "medical" experience at the hospice first and then highlight my extracurricular activities.

I met Kathryn Mannix at the start of my 2nd week. She was exhausted from a week spent in France with thousands of handicapped children and had to assume the reins of the hospice, as Claud was away for one week. I finally sat down with her on Wednesday to discuss my objectives and means for meeting such. We had pleasantly interacted until that juncture, whereupon we connected on numerous levels. I was able to establish specific objectives for the different dimensions of palliative medicine as I viewed it from outside - the physical, emotional, psychological, and spiritual components to the human experience of terminal illness. Can there be any other area of medicine that allows such holism? To this set of objectives was added the objective of experiencing the different types of care utilized to palliate distress in any of these components

I was assigned a small case load and became manager of these patients. My first patient was a 50 year old woman with metastatic breast cancer who was undergoing chemotherapy. I will avoid becoming clinical and will not give you her case history. I was given the challenge of deciding upon and implementing a treatment plan for this lady, who was the first patient they ever admitted for palliation of primarily psychological distress. She has a long history of agoraphobia and panic attacks and had not been coping at home due to numerous factors, the most pressing of which was her impending chemotherapy after her last chemotherapy session resulted in very nasty side-effects. I began some informal counselling and relaxation sessions with her. It was absolutely beautiful. She went home after 2 weeks, having undergone chemotherapy and in a more stable state with controlled anxiety and some strategy for the immediate future. I was privileged to have been involved and this experience - specific experience - will prove quite monumental in the future, I believe. Somehow I was given the ability to help her help herself when much of the rest of the staff were tremendously anxious about admitting her. Praise be to the holy inexplicable.

My experiences at the hospice continued to grow. During the third week, Claud was back but Kathryn was on study leave and the other ward physician was off. Therefore, I became the ward doctor in essence and I experienced the strange reversal from "nurse auxiliary" to "physician" status. This was interesting and will add to my collection of experiences that will impinge on my role as a physician in the future (other experiences being: the patient, the family member of a patient, hospital volunteer supervisor, nurse auxiliary...)

This hospice functions in a multivariate and different way than I had anticipated. I will not go into detail here, other than to say that its approach is better than my outside conception, and I believe much of others', both professional and non, conceptions. I have so many ideas for the future - I hope I am granted the facility to pursue as many as possible and maintain my ideals. I also hope to go to sleep soon, but want to finish this letter. I am also losing my clarity of and motivation for thought. I will write a little more and then say adieu pour maintenant and finish tomorrow morning.

I need to explain my connectedness with Kathryn. She is a reasonably radical Christian like me, has an absurd sense of humour, is extremely loving, has enchanting green eyes, and is married to a wonderful and very unpretentious pathologist. I cannot explain any further, especially at this hour, except that I cannot imagine ever having such a crucial mission fulfilled in such a truly beautiful manner. That is it - my experience dans Newcastle was filled with beauty. Beauty is such a rare thing, and yet it surrounded me... beautiful pain, beautiful relief, beautiful life, beautiful death, beautiful people. In happiness and sadness, in disharmony and harmony there was beauty. This all sounds terribly profound - and it was, but there was also much silliness (good old take your head off and jump up and down silliness)

89.05.0

I must finish this thing. It's Saturday morning and I'm sitting in l'Hotel de Ville (city hall) at the reception centre. I'm supposed to be singing with a few thousand others who are practising for the massed choir finale tonight, but I would rather be violently ill than scream with them for 2 hours. As soon as I am finished this I will explore Nancy and all of its lovely parameters

An interesting example of the meaningfulness of my experience in Newcastle comes in the form of a simple question. I quickly learned how to ask "how are you?" and actually mean it. This simple question provided more information than any other. It would be interesting to apply this to every day life and our dealings with one another. It is also interesting that in France the question "a vu?" holds more significance for me as well - perhaps this is because it is a novel language.

The number of meaningful relationships that were established for me, both with patients and non-patients, was astounding. Many of these went beyond the bounds of superficial friendships. Five weeks was sufficiently long for me to become involved with beautiful people, fully integrate into the team at the hospice, gain important experience in the field, and decide on this area of medicine for my future. It was also long enough for me to expand my horizons and feel frustrated at not being able to remain and develop and grow and enjoy my new environment. This is, I believe, a good way to leave - with a new set of objectives for the future, with much motivation, with much satisfaction, and with much sadness. I leave to come back again (in the not too distant future); and I leave with great thankfulness for a most blessed experience. The most difficult element was saying goodbye to the specific few with whom I shared my soul and, more importantly, to the patients on the ward, where my goodbye was poignantly final and again more than a mere passing statement. There is more, but it will remain unsaid.

My second weekend was again spent in Newcastle. Saturday I attended a football watch with Kathryn's husband Chris and gained an authentic Newcastle experience - the lost, I stood in the end zone terraces (similar to those in Hillsborough where the disaster occurred), and cold rain poured down on us part way through. I enjoyed every minute. Sunday I attended a morning service with two significant people, Pam, who is a community nurse stationed at the hospice and her husband Mervin. The afternoon was composed of a thorough and marvellously information overloaded tour of Newcastle by an official tour guide. He does some volunteer work at the hospice and, even though the walking tours do not begin until the end of May, offered me a personal and comprehensive touring history of the city. I spent the evening with Kathryn and Chris after attending mass with them. I already mentioned seeing Don Giovanni, which sounds similar to seeing the Messiah, earlier in that week.

My 3rd weekend was spent in Cambridge with Sue and Stephen and was extraordinary, which is to say that it has been consistent with everything else. Saturday we (re)explored Ely and Sunday we walked around the colleges. It is very gratifying to tread upon already known paths, with both old and fresh memories involved. What a splendid mix between interactions with remarkable people and completely independent explorations this journey has been. I could not imagine having travelled in any way but by myself. The internal conversations and running narrative have been fascinating and, of course, blend consistently into the narrative that is my life.

My final weekend, before my final week, was perfectly appropriate. Saturday I travelled with Pam and Mervin and another younger couple up the NE coast to Holy Island - a most holy island, where St. Cuthbert lived and where St. Aidan established a monastery, which was the focus for the meeting of Celtic and Roman Christianity. I have experienced no more misty and mystical environment than this area. Sunday I toured the Lake District with a nurse tutor who had visited the hospice for 2 weeks from Devon. It was absolutely sensuous and at once spiritual. I was unfortunately unable to visit Julie in Birmingham, but sent her a card promising that I would visit during my next trip to England (next year). To complete the circle of the magical mystery and spiritual history tour, I revisited Durham Cathedral during my final week, heard evensong, and had time for reflection at the tombs of St. Cuthbert and the most venerable Bede. At Christmas, when I was given Bede's Ecclesiastical History, I presumed that I would spend my time in London. I ended up in the darkest heart of Bede's land without knowing so until I arrived. Praise be to God for dapple-down-drawn things

So my journey in England is complete save for a few hours between flights. (In actuality, my journey in England is just beginning.) It is with gladness and sadness that I leave. France has been superb. I will not say much here. The choir has perhaps captured the community's imagination and appreciation more than any other and is certainly second to none in performance (this is by far the best I have ever heard them). I leave for Germany tomorrow and with great anticipation. There is a chance I may not come home next Friday, by which time you may not have received this, but I believe this will be more in mind than body.

Au revoir et cher,
Glenn

Postcard of lions
Kapsowar, Kenya
89.10.11

Dear Mum and Dad,

Once again the touch from loving parents: I received the unfortunate telegram tonight and have written Michael. Yours was an appropriate selection of words. I hope my bumblings were appropriate for Michael. I feel quite distanced physically, but perhaps more attached spiritually (once again). As they say, "absence makes the soul grow stronger". I will say nothing more of the death of baby Julie - for there is little to say and much to think and feel. (Except that I reaffirm my thought that in all death there exists some sort of absolute beauty.)

I have much to express now, and have had time to reflect on my initial and wonderful confusion upon entering this utterly "not mine" land (perhaps I have become the astronaut of my fantasy and have landed on a different planet).

The hour is late in the mystery of night in the Kenyan highlands. I will write soon with stories and thoughts. But for now at least I have finally written from this extraordinary experience.

Love,
Glenn

Kapsowar Hospital
Box 130
Eldoret, Kenya
where am I?
89.10.14

Dear Mum and Dad,

...and so a letter, finally, and written on this autumn afternoon, where the leaves have changed from green to green, and the sky has opened for a moment of spring renewal, not long enough to moisten the African songs of birds outside my window, where the warm shadows lengthen and the clouds reveal peace and give mist to the layers of mountains and ridges that form a changing horizon over the valley where night now exists and creeps its black fingers through the forest towards my feet. Summer begins this autumn day and yet to me continues, though the leaves change to green. If I were to descend, with the night, into the valley below my shadows, my heart in darkness would beat somewhat deeper and I, myself as well, would choke on black air within the heart of darkest darkness. This paper, now shrouded in darkness, is not the darkness of which I speak. And speak so quietly - yet I must wait now for light, even with this shadow of night upon my hill.

I cannot see now, as I write - where is the light - I demand my light! Am I alone in this darkness, this pseudo-darkness? The horizon dims. I must hold my paper up to my familiar window (and still there is not enough light). The leaves change from green to black in the horrible autumn night of this darkness. I cannot enter this darkness - what if the valley came with it? I'll close my eyes to shut out darkness. I see a light deep in the valley, and it is gone. The flash of a white man's torch, no doubt. Where are the fires to warm the black valley dwellers? I cannot see. This is not my heart of darkness to enter. I realize the plunge into darkness, but this is not my plunge... So I wait for light.

I can wait no longer. By the light of this paraffin lamp the autumn night regains peace and my fears disappear with the horizon. Why does my white skin not glow so as to provide the light I need? At least my writing is clearer.

89.10.18

It has been many years from my last sitting for this letter. Perhaps I thought that I was changing, developing, becoming increasingly profound with the journey of my last sitting. Perhaps I thought I was alive and traversing some thrilling edge of life. Perhaps I thought I sensed darkness. With no perhaps - I was the fool. I must use "perhaps" in speaking of my past, for it is a past I have forever lost in these intervening years. So I will speculate about that past and then, perhaps (for my future is as dissociated from my frozen present), I will speak with cut out tongue of true darkness and hopefully I will be blessed with the ability to weep in my speaking.

(And may I never cease to weep. Amen.)

First, how can I continue to use "I" when I, I believe, that is to say the past I, no longer exists. It was not destroyed, but rather absorbed in some way much beyond me.

Second, I, the amorphous one, will choose to continue with the device called "I". Third, I apologize for this crypticism. Never again will there be clarity, especially the artificial sort spoken of at the unplanned ending of my first sitting.

Fourth, I continue with perhaps previously mentioned (on a journey long ago through the land of mystical shadows and beautiful malignant dying) obsession for completeness of some sort. This time not a cataloguing of events and reflections, but rather the ruminating thoughts and feelings of the corporeal spirit called I. I must attempt to complete these circles without endings.

Now, to speculate about and perhaps touch the ideas from the last sitting - that irrecoverable past. (What a joke this exercise is, in view of frozen present and its sleepless movements...do you know that I can still laugh and joke and be absurd - how absurd!) I am white, you see, a bloodless, pale sort. I have power (in my whiteness). This is great power / stay out of the valley. I can command, even save (of course save / kill?) the black ones, and live in power with my other whites / avoid the valley. I can eat chocolate desserts or ugali / beware the valley.

I cannot be here, my skin scares some children and represents the vehicle for begging to many adults and so on, ad nauseum...adventitia pulmonica...agnus dei qui tollis peccata mundi, miserere nobis. You see, the black ones, the Kenyans, the Marakwet, my co-workers, my patients, the patients, the others, can wear white and say "brother in Jesus..." and wash my white (well, more muddy) socks, but I forget to ask if I might visit and mention a faith important to me (but 97.58% of Kenyans are Christian - let us move on, whips in hand, and tackle those damned - and I mean damned - penguins in the Antarctic now!) I am confused; I am tired (I have never been tired before). Let me leave this thought, its simple anger and casual impetus, its past, so many years ago from last Saturday. Let me weep, please.

Intellectually I know that I have crossed beyond my emotional means - it does not matter how far, once you have crossed. Somehow I still possess some emotional energy - it is not from I. You see, Sunday night I ceased to exist. It is completely ironic - I write you Wednesday night as the hour approaches ten, the lights begin to dim as the hospital generator shuts off for the day, the melancholic music in my ears comes to a close, and it has begun to rain outside my room. Thus, my paraffin lamp is lit in anticipation of the false darkness which shrouded my first strange sitting. Let me then continue and speak of what is perhaps true darkness (written exactly as the lights extinguish - I must move the lamp closer). The Holy Spirit continues to weep on my behalf outside. I do not ask for pity. I only ask to speak and grieve and perhaps to stay here and visit a little longer.

I have seen my death mask.

Unfortunately it was worn by a beautiful (absolutely beautiful) girl of 2 years of age. Her soul is now free... I suspect her mother's imprisoned... mine sustained only by inexplicable grace. I pray for her soul, and for the souls of others, and for my soul, and for mother's and for mothers. (Now, Glenn - a name I once answered to - is there scriptural support for praying for the souls of the dead? Fuck off.) I apologize only that it was not my soul freed. I wish it had been, for it was my death mask. My eyes close with exhaustion - would that they had pennies on them and my veins filled with plastic. I outwardly contradict my inward cowardice with such absurd statements. Ashes to ashes and dusk to dawn - I must sleep soon and dream of grief (I have two dreams to relate in a different segment of this letter. In reality my present stupor, or lack of weeping, prevents me from allowing this entire letter to appear as a plea for psychiatric evaluation - in actuality, it is the furthest thing from that).

I think I do disservice to continue. I have lost inspiration in this sitting and must once again retire to sleep without having wept. I am the corporeal and yawn excessively. I was allowed only three hours sleep last night while on call and had been up (down?) for many years. It is half past ten.

89.10.27

Where am I (once again)? It has been quite a while since my second sitting on this interminable letter - I believe I have said that of my letters before - I also believe I have never written one like this one. It is almost two weeks since I began these flights of ideas and hopefully tomorrow I can send them on their way to flying home. I am sorry about my lack of correspondence. It is not for lack of desire or for lack of stuff to transmit by letter. I have received news of the Blue Jays conquest and fall (and am satisfied with the conquest). I have received the sad, but oh so properly written and expressed, telegram. I have received a postcard from my second home from the beautiful Becky. I have received an enjoyable picture of a cow and good news of the beautiful Bev. I have received details of Julie Root's death and of the other Roots' life and have been almost touched in my separation from that other reality of my life elsewhere. (A reality, no doubt, that will retain some separateness and a developing newness in the future or whatever.) I have received word that I did not arrive in Nairobi - I may not have, I can't remember, but I certainly am here on this distant planet, wherever it is. By the way, I and Joanne arrived at Nairobi as scheduled and I phoned Fred Aluda, as instructed, who was not home, as unexpected. I searched the airport, which is not a difficult task, tried to look as white as possible and resemble my graduation picture (easier then than now), and found no evidence of his existence. The holy inexplicable one was present, I guess, and manifested in two young women from "AIM serve" with my name on a sign. Thus, I was safely transported to my initial destination that opening African night - the show has been running non-stop for 5 weeks now. Of course, I was told before I left that "AIM serve" could not possibly help with transport. I phoned Fred throughout the weekend without answer, but will attempt to contact him at the end (is it possible - the end?) of my African adventure before I continue what may be a most longterm adventure in England. I also received a letter yesterday detailing many things about my beautiful family and the special people at First Baptist (by the way, "family" certainly includes persons such as Tyler and Kevin and Rosemary and Bev and Pete and Michael...). I have envisioned presenting my slides and some of my story at First some evening for those who are interested if it would be meaningful for the church.

This does not preclude any gestures that I will make to the remarkable people who have sponsored me on this adventure and all of its many darknesses (and subsequent lights).

How very strange, in the midst of much strangeness this letter must present to you, to have such a ray of hope interjected. I believe that if there is to be light, there must be darkness first. Perhaps if there is hope, there must be despair, utter despair, to precede. And if there exists true self, in any sense, there must be destruction of self to begin. I may have learned something of dying to self - certainly if I speak much here, I obviously have learned little. I don't know, perhaps I cling desperately to the false self for survival (but rather death). I am not sure - on this I cannot reflect. I will not tread into the "I" business again. I do promise consistency, however, with regard to crypticism. Thank goodness, the lights have gone out (10 p.m. you know), and I continue with the rumination of my thoughts. I cannot describe details of my experiences to this point, for I would need two minutes to write for every minute lived here (where? the theme persists).

> So I have seen my death mask worn
> on the face of another -
> a beautiful, small African girl.

Three Mondays ago she came to hospital gravely ill (the divine darkness does foreshadow). I saw her with Dr. Ann and we suspected a bowel obstruction and decided to watch her for a few hours, knowing full well that an operation was at hand. (Also knowing that no surgeon was here and danger loomed ahead.) So we operated late in the afternoon. Do I need mention shadows and darkness?

We, Dr. Ann and I, opened her abdomen and the grossly distended bowel jumped out. We relieved the obstruction as best as possible in hopes that she could survive to the arrival of the Canadian surgeon the upcoming Saturday. It was then, with the obstruction at least temporarily not a concern, that we began to pray, and I for the first time ever. The damned bowel was too distended to push back inside! We tried everything at our disposal, save excision of some bowel and almost certain homicide with that. Oh God - why did we choose to operate? I could have almost laughed because the situation was so unreal. I could have laughed except that just prior to the operation, as the nurses and Dr. Ann prepared, I stood with this child and held her arms gently and stroked her small head as she breathed unnaturally (I cannot adequately describe this breathing) and progressively closed her eyes, only to startle and stare into my eyes with her tormented ones. She stared into my very soul and pleader for life, knowing much more of the situation than any of us. She stared into my soul with her dying eyes and I was the child and she the old spirit and it hurt. So I did not laugh.

(One cannot express oneself adequately, ever.)

One cannot express oneself adequately when one is weeping with words on paper.

We decided to give her deep anaesthesia, hoping that the abdomen would relax and we could place the bowel back from whence it came. The clinical officer assisting (clinical officer is somewhere in training between nurse and junior doctor) gave her the anaesthesia and intubated. I knew something was amiss, listened to the child's chest immediately and discovered that the esophagus as opposed to the trachea had been intubated, and ripped the tube out of her little mouth. She was completely paralysed and not breathing as a result. So I began to resuscitate, while holding her head with my now contaminated and blood stained hands. I resuscitated until the anaesthesia wore off and she began to breathe spontaneously. It is remarkable what one can do without thought and with, in fact only with, divine mediation. Dr. Ann and I rescrubbed and returned to our nemesis, the bowel. I don't understand what happened, said one who irrationally took the leap of faith, but nothing had changed and we simply placed the bowel back into the abdomen; my hands, Dr. Ann's hands, the scrub nurse's hands, and the Holy Spirit's hands.

Tea-time! I'm back with tea, a scone and two antimalarial tablets. I continue.

The child, Beatrice, survived the week with much careful attention, antibiotics, and the else. Saturday, Dr. Mighton arrived straight from someplace called Hamilton, Ontario, in Canada. He is 71 years old, just retired from the Hamilton General in July, and I will describe him no further for fear of letting many descriptive details into my written ruminations.

I was on call Saturday night and was awakened from sleep by a knock and a note at 6 a.m. Sunday. The child was ill with abdominal distension and a fever. She looked extremely sick and indeed was. I assessed her and called for Dr. Ann and

Dr. Mighton. At 3 p.m. we began surgery, with Ann watching anaesthesia and myself assisting Dr. Mighton. He did an excellent and exquisite job. Beatrice was to be almost my entire Sabbath (unless you're Jewish, 7th Day Adventist, or just don't care, in which case it would be Sunday), from my waking to a C-section delivery before my next sleeping. Bible study, a quite stimulating one at that, had just ended with people munching on munchies and sipping from hot mugs, when a message came for Ann that Beatrice was breathing poorly and looked even more poorly. It was approaching 10 p.m. Sunday night of the longest day of my life or the longest night of my death. Dr. Mighton and Dr. Ann headed off. I finished my hot chocolate and went home, brushed my teeth, and was about to put my pyjamas on when I was told (I use this particular word out of convenience) to go to the hospital. Praise be to the holy inexplicable. Praise be to the holy horrible. So I walked and ran briskly with a purpose that was not self ordained.

There she was, without breathing, the beautiful one. Before the operation earlier, she had peered into my soul once more. I had stroked her head and held her hand, but she breathed softly then. There was no great distress despite her sad condition. She looked up at me with no whimper, only dry tears. She knew so much. I know nothing.

> Here we go 'round the operating table
> Here we go 'round the operating table
> Here we go 'round the operating table
> at 3 o'clock in the afternoon
> This is the way (her) life ends
> This is the way (her) life ends
> This is the way (my) life ends
> Not with a bang and not with a whimper.
> Our Father...

There I was transported to the scene of her, with Ann and Dr. Mighton hovering around, squeezing the bag to give her air. "Is it going in?" I asked. They didn't know. "Any spontaneous breaths?" They didn't think so. "Perhaps the tetany could be due to hypocalcemia", I eulogized. They hadn't thought of that. "Let me listen to her chest", I said in benediction. There was no air entry of worth. I pulled the mask and bag off her beautiful face and began to blow my air in. She could not look into my soul now and I could not breathe deeply enough to reach hers. Ann left because a woman in labour was having seizures. Dr. Mighton didn't know what to do. I breathed my breaths into her and I breathed my breaths into her and I....I gave her calcium IV now. Her face and hands were in spasm and gradually began to relax. The nurse handed me the oxygen mask and I said no good. This was not the mask for me. I breathed my breaths into her. Her face relaxed, giving it peace (peace?), and the mask began to form. I breathed my breaths...Her pupils were fixed and dilated... I breathed... "I will (puff) continue until (puff) her heart stops (puff)".....I.....no heart sounds, silent face, dead face.....I?

I listened and looked and checked and pronounced clinically dead. "Dr. Mighton, go get Ann." My hands trembled as I cradled her beautiful body. I pulled all the tubes out and cleaned the body. Her death mask remained - it was mine.
I have seen my death mask.

Ann came and told one of the nurses to inform the mother of her beautiful child's death. I told Ann that we should go with the nurse. I told the nurse to tell the mother that her child had died and we could do nothing. The nurse told the mother in Kalenjin. Mother cried. The relatives came in and cried. We stood in the room and let them cry. After a few minutes of eternity, I asked the nurse to inform the mother that we had to leave and that we would and did pray. We walked to maternity and delivered the baby from the fitting woman. My mind was empty. I went to bed. Someday I will wake up, and maybe I too will cry.
I have nothing more to say. I had nothing to say when I began this letter, and have said nothing through it.

(That is my prayer of nothingness.)

The following Tuesday I was on call and about to go to bed, when a knock came and soon I was walking to the pediatric ward (the ward of Sunday night). I am losing energy at this time or writing, by want to finish.

I entered the back room and there was the child, with brain oozing out the right side of his head. I stood still at the door, briefly considered death, and knelt beside the child who lay on his father's lap. This 6 year old boy had been inadvertently hit in the head with a stick used during cow-herding that evening. His brain pulsated. His vital signs were stable and he was responsive to painful stimuli. I called the operating room staff, sent someone to turn the generator on, called for Dr. Mighton and Dr. Ann, and told the parents that it would be a good idea to pray, for the situation was grim. I quickly read about some radical measures to employ in situations of severe head injury and we operated. The child, Barnaba, has some left-sided weakness, but is able to move his limbs, has walked a little bit, and today I tickled him and we both smiled (he looking more cute with his white bandaged head). This is a miracle. At the risk of being redundant, this is a miracle.

After darkness, there is some light. I have not wept, but my tears have been wiped away. I have experienced more in these five weeks than in a lifetime. Four days in a row last week, I was involved in resuscitating patients who had either respiratory or cardiac arrests. Two lived and two died. I have done an incredible number of things that I never would have thought possible or that I would be capable of doing. I have met these Kenyans and thought and felt much. I have grown to have meaningful relationships with many of the staff/missionaries here. I am continually awestruck by the absolute beauty of this land. I spent last Saturday climbing a mountain. I have walked down into the valley and by the river by myself. I have spent sacred time both with myself and without myself. I have sensed the holy inexplicable at many junctions. I have sung a duet in church with a British medical student and had the text read in Kalenjin beforehand.

I must close this letter. I will tell you of a dream or two in the next correspondence (must be the high altitude that alters my sleeping mind so).

Love,
Glenn

Nairobi, Kenya
89.11.10

Dear Mum and Dad,

... so the adventure continues, having changed location as of today. I have a few of these aerograms to use, so I will attempt to compartmentalize my written meanderings to match the space provided.

First, to some unfinished business: before I forget it entirely, I should like to relate one of my altitudinally-bizarre dreams. It was set in prehistoric times, but rather than the Rift Valley, it was along the banks of the ancient Thames in location. Kenyan jungle surrounded these grassy banks, as young mzonga ("white") children skateboarded up and down the cement sidewalks. The Thames flowed steadily but peacefully through the corrugated tin tubes that formed waterways beneath stone bridges (like those arching over the river Cam in Cambridge). Various dinosaurs roamed about, munching on the vegetation and appearing quite oblivious to anything by their lumbering ways. There were no vicious carnivores or swooping nasties from the sky.

Life was pleasant, if not benign, in this most green setting along the then young Thames. Our family inhabited one of the trees which bent its trunk over the river in a gentle curve that was most conducive for setting up house. We appeared much the same as we would at present, including typical attire and methods of behaviour. And so life progressed in this anachronistic dream land.

At one point, however, I heard a sound more massive and musical than any dinosaur fart. It was the organ of Westminster Abbey booming across the prehistoric Thames. (It did not disturb the dinos.) Someone was playing a composer's, whose name escapes me now (Patricia Phillips used to play some of his stuff), variation on Bach's "Wachet Auf". I, of course, assumed it was Dad, having decided to use his nimble fingers on the grand organ across the banks. Mum corrected me, though, explaining that it was John Laing playing. "Oh," I said and then turned to watch the little boys skateboard past the dinosaurs while organ music continued to echo over the London jungle.

Love,
Glenn

Nairobi, Kenya
89.11.14

Dear Mum and Dad,

I'm back in Nairobi from safari and will depart for England late tonight (actually early tomorrow). (I will here use a word I tend to dislike, but it is most appropriate in description.) Mount Kilimanjaro is awesome. We camped near its base and had elephants roaming through the grounds while sleeping at night. I was up each morning before you were going to bed the day before - i.e, at about 5:30 a.m. It will be better to relate stories of the animals, my impressions, and the setting, with pictures when I arrive home. I saw all the animals I hoped to except for lions. This afternoon I plan on going to Nairobi National park to see them and some of the others.

"I had another dream..." (Martin Luther Glenn)...the night before I left for safari. I was at the hotel from which I wrote aerogram 1. I will be brief: it was set within Dickens' A Christmas Carol with Alistair Sim and the classic production. I was present in this black and white setting, but only a passive observer. It was not the whole story, but rather some sort of complete in itself excerpt version. In the end - the final scene of my dream - Scrooge visits his nephew's house at the singing of "Barbara Allen" This is a haunting tune which I can never remember, but I woke up the next morning with it in my mind and walked the streets of Nairobi, on my way to pay for the safari and get my sleeping bag, singing the beautiful "Barbara Allen". It was most pleasant. I remember the tonic solfa now, though I can't quite piece the tune together...oh, to wait for another dream.

Presently I am awaiting Fred Aluda, who will take me around Nairobi this morning and will have Joanne and myself to supper before we head to the airport this evening. There was a message from him for me here at Mayfield Guesthouse when I arrived yesterday. I was worried that something could have been wrong at home (which was not pleasant), but Fred had found out when I was returning and was most insistent that I contact him. It's good to be taken care of.

This is my final aerogram. The theme here encompasses some parting reflections on Kapsowar. I was most sad to leave - more sad than any elective before (hence, I guess, "most" sad). I was able and allowed to do so much medically, but I was also living in a community of Christian people, both missionary and natives, some of whom I have come to care about quite deeply. I was not prepared to leave (not that I usually am from such experiences).

Sunday afternoon, Ann (Dr. Fursdon) and myself went on an extraordinary and taxing walk through the valleys and hills. Two natives met up with us late in the afternoon and with little comprehension on our part, urged us to join them on an adventure through the bush and down a steep valley edge to a hidden waterfall. They showed us their water supply, the rock where they (or rather the women) make millet flour, and how to trap small animals with rocks. These black people took me into their heart of darkness and there was much light. I do not know them / we spoke no common words / they are my friends / I am their friend / there is Truth in darkness approached faithfully / I gave them 5 k.sh. each.

Ann and I have gone through more than I can ever relate to you. Charles (Dr. Millson) and I had that divinely ordained mode of communication, even though he was away for 4 weeks of my time. Dr. Mighton (the Canadian and Hamilton surgeon) was my parent and my child. My final night in Kapsowar, though I think I have carried Kapsowar with me these past few nights, I lay in bed and felt what seemed too much love for these people, as well as others in my life - especially family. I have never felt this before. It was too difficult.

I almost did not make it to Nairobi on Friday, as our jeep had broken down coming back from a dispensary trip in the valley on Thursday. I started packing late and did not want to leave. It is good, though.

Wednesday,(prior), Charles and I worked together at the hospital - my last working day there. A 2 year old boy died after surgery for a huge abdominal tumour. We tried and tried to resuscitate. We prayed with the parents for the child's soul and for them (and for us?) I did not weep, and yet I think I did. It continues. I am content and I am disturbed.

Love,
Glenn

Mother's Note

Glenn was a man of specific passions, not the least of which was his love of English literature. It was his own writing ability, his need to stay here as long as possible for his family, his music, his vast belief system and his concern for humanity that kept his soul robust beyond what most would have believed humanly possible. Glenn would probably have said, "It was not humanly possible; I did not do it myself." As 2009 progressed and the enemy moved on relentlessly, Glenn stated that he felt utterly at one with the Holy Spirit, so much so that, a few days before his collapse on October 29, he wrote in an email, "Hi Mum, Boy, am I content!"

The utmost, though least wanted, honour of my lifetime has been to assemble this book for Mary.

Excerpt from *invISibility vISibyllized*

are you there? here? are
you the shorewaves grandeur of our Huron,
the seasons of your beloved service berry tree in your
home garden,
the voice of theodora when she sings and astonishes
in her absoluteness of pitch, are you
the voice of her finger-
tips releasing the music that wants to live, are you her
colours of quavers and her kinship with the music
of the spheres? and are you her sanguine
approach to this often chaotic planet?

are you there? here? are
you as visible as the wind, your fre-
quency now so high we can only see or feel the
effect... if we apply intent as straight as
the flight of an ancient quiver? are
you the insatiable appetite of henry to
know everything, invent and recreate, to file allworthiness
in the microchip chambers of his Dickinson
brain, are we talking about the sound of
silence and do you heft
things as syllables of sound?

are you there? here? are
you the continuance of familiar and elegant
gestures, the imprint where Mary gains strength
in resting, the new resident in her
soul where the two of you live in the
immaterial, where your one soul is
sustained by the speed of
light, the absence of
time?

yes. you are. there. here
in the running dialogue of our souls, in the
ephemeral touch on my shoulder, the voice
that is forever accessible if I listen beyond
silence.

and i know that this was somehow meant to
be, but i dare go no further. for words are chaff
thrown into the wind when it comes to the feebleness of
descriptions in the Kingdom
of Broken Asunder Bonds. Is it then
Narnia where you
are?

Ellyn Peirson
July 22, 2010

About the author:

Glenn Peirson walked boldly and compassionately in this world, blazing new pathways, dreaming new dreams into being, and maintaining beautiful relationships. The complications of cancer treatment suddenly claimed him in November, 2009, after a three year heroic battle. His deepest devotion was to his God and his family: his wife, Dr. Mary Peirson; his twelve year old daughter, Theodora; and his nine year old son, Henry.

Glenn was born in Kingston, Ontario, and raised in Guelph. He was a scholar, athlete, musician, spiritual giant, poet, gardener and great lover of the Land of Narnia. Before he completed secondary school, he was admitted on scholarship to the University of Guelph. During this time he was tenor soloist at Metropolitan United Church in Toronto. He received research grants, in particular, an NSERC grant in brain laterality and music. He was the Winegard Gold-Medalist at his convocation.

Glenn went immediately from his studies to McMaster Medical School in Hamilton, Ontario. In the entire period of medical school and residency, he sang with the celebrated Tafelmusik Baroque Orchestra's Chamber Choir, Toronto. Glenn also created practicums that took him to Moose Factory and further north, to Kapsowar in Kenya, and to St. Oswald's Hospice in Newcastle-upon-Tyne in England. It was in his residency at McMaster that he met and fell in love with Mary Beingessner, who had studied medicine at the University of Toronto. They married in 1991, in their final year of residency and while Glenn was Chief Resident. In 1992, they spent two months in Malaysia, running a preventative medicine research project they had designed.

Glenn and Mary moved to Guelph in 1994. Mary established her career in public health medicine. Glenn worked as a palliative care physician, a community health centre physician and, in 1999, established a private practice in Cambridge, near Guelph. He was also the addictions medicine physician at Stonehenge Therapeutic Community. He maximized a life-style that included time for his highly cherished home-life, his music, his faith and finally his writing. He was a founding member of Tactus Vocal Ensemble, and a wine and spa writer for North American Inns magazine.

Finding and encouraging artistic gifts in children was a great joy for Glenn. His children have participated abundantly in the Guelph Youth Singers, Operetta Camp, the Kiwanis Festival and the Southern Ontario Suzuki Institute's summer program at Laurier University. He was a vital member of Dublin Street United Church in Guelph, relishing it as a spiritual community for his family and as a place of spiritual growth and healing for all who attended. Our friend Evelyn once said, "Dublin Church is the platform for the articulation of Glenn's soul."

Glenn's spirit continues to be strong. As he said, with a gentle touch, to every patient at the end of an appointment: "Be well."

website: www.physicianmusician.com